Native American religion /
J 299.7 Bon 6989355
Bonvillain, Nancy.
Smyrna Public Library

D0928091

WITHDRAWN

Smyrna Public Library
100 Village Green Circle
Smyrna, GA 30080

NATIVE AMERICAN RELIGION

Smyrna Public Library
100 Village Green Circle
Smyrna, GA 30080

INDIANS OF NORTH AMERICA

NATIVE AMERICAN RELIGION

Nancy Bonvillain
New School for Social Research

Frank W. Porter III
General Editor

CHELSEA HOUSE PUBLISHERS
New York Philadelphia

On the cover A Pawnee drum from the 1890s, used in a vision-inspired game that formed part of a Ghost Dance ceremony.
Frontispiece A rattle used in peyote ceremonies, made of gourd, beads, sinews, and feathers.

Chelsea House Publishers
Editorial Director Richard Rennert
Executive Managing Editor Karyn Gullen Browne
Copy Chief Robin James
Picture Editor Adrian G. Allen
Creative Director Robert Mitchell
Art Director Joan Ferrigno
Production Manager Sallye Scott

Indians of North America
Senior Editor Sean Dolan
Native American Specialist Jack Miller

***Staff for* NATIVE AMERICAN RELIGION**
Assistant Editor Mary B. Sisson
Designer Cambraia Magalhaes
Picture Researcher Matthew Dudley

Copyright © 1996 by Chelsea House Publishers, a division of Main Line Book Co. All rights reserved. Printed and bound in the United States of America.

3 5 7 9 8 6 4 2

Library of Congress Cataloging-in-Publication Data

Bonvillain, Nancy.
Native American religion / Nancy Bonvillain ; Frank W. Porter III, general editor.
p. cm.—(Indians of North America)
Includes bibliographical references and index.
Summary: Surveys the various religions of different groups of Native Americans.
ISBN 0-7910-2652-3.
0-7910-3479-8 (pbk.)
1. Indians of North America—Religion—Juvenile literature. [1. Indians of North America—Religion.] I. Porter, Frank W., 1947- . II. Title. III. Series: Indians of North America (Chelsea House Publishers).
E98.R3865 1995 95-2157
299'.7—dc20 CIP
AC

CONTENTS

INDIANS OF NORTH AMERICA

The Abenaki
The Apache
The Arapaho
The Archaeology of North America
The Aztecs
The Blackfoot
The Cahuilla
The Catawbas
The Cherokee
The Cheyenne
The Chickasaw
The Chinook
The Chipewyan
The Choctaw
The Chumash
The Coast Salish Peoples
The Comanche
The Creeks
The Crow
Federal Indian Policy
The Hidatsa
The Hopi
The Huron
The Innu
The Inuit
The Iroquois
The Kiowa
The Kwakiutl
The Lenapes
Literatures of the American Indian
The Lumbee
The Maya
The Menominee
The Modoc
The Mohawk
The Nanticoke
The Narragansett
The Navajos
The Nez Perce
The Ojibwa
The Osage
The Paiute
The Pawnee
The Pima-Maricopa
The Potawatomi
The Powhatan Tribes
The Pueblo
The Quapaws
The Sac and Fox
The Santee Sioux
The Seminole
The Shawnee
The Shoshone
The Tarahumara
The Teton Sioux
The Tunica-Biloxi
Urban Indians
The Wampanoag
Women in American Indian Society
The Yakima
The Yankton Sioux
The Yuma
The Zuni

CHELSEA HOUSE PUBLISHERS

INDIANS OF NORTH AMERICA: CONFLICT AND SURVIVAL

Frank W. Porter III

The Indians survived our open intention of wiping them out, and since the tide turned they have even weathered our good intentions toward them, which can be much more deadly.

John Steinbeck
America and Americans

When Europeans first reached the North American continent, they found hundreds of tribes occupying a vast and rich country. The newcomers quickly recognized the wealth of natural resources. They were not, however, so quick or willing to recognize the spiritual, cultural, and intellectual riches of the people they called Indians.

The Indians of North America examines the problems that develop when people with different cultures come together. For American Indians, the consequences of their interaction with non-Indian people have been both productive and tragic. The Europeans believed they had "discovered" a "New World," but their religious bigotry, cultural bias, and materialistic world view kept them from appreciating and understanding the people who lived in it. All too often they attempted to change the way of life of the indigenous people. The Spanish conquistadores wanted the Indians as a source of labor. The Christian missionaries, many of whom were English, viewed them as potential converts. French traders and trappers used the Indians as a means to obtain pelts. As Francis Parkman, the 19th-century historian, stated, "Spanish civilization crushed the Indian; English civilization scorned and neglected him; French civilization embraced and cherished him."

Nearly 500 years later, many people think of American Indians as curious vestiges of a distant past, waging a futile war to survive in a Space Age society. Even today, our understanding of the history and culture of American Indians is too often derived from unsympathetic, culturally biased, and inaccurate reports. The American Indian, described and portrayed in thousands of movies, television programs, books, articles, and government studies, has either been raised to the status of the "noble savage" or disparaged as the "wild Indian" who resisted the westward expansion of the American frontier.

Where in this popular view are the real Indians, the human beings and communities whose ancestors can be traced back to ice-age hunters? Where are the creative and indomitable people whose sophisticated technologies used the natural resources to ensure their survival, whose military skill might even have prevented European settlement of North America if not for devastating epidemics and disruption of the ecology? Where are the men and women who are today diligently struggling to assert their legal rights and express once again the value of their heritage?

The various Indian tribes of North America, like people everywhere, have a history that includes population expansion, adaptation to a range of regional environments, trade across wide networks, internal strife, and warfare. This was the reality. Europeans justified their conquests, however, by creating a mythical image of the New World and its native people. In this myth, the New World was a virgin land, waiting for the Europeans. The arrival of Christopher Columbus ended a timeless primitiveness for the original inhabitants.

Also part of this myth was the debate over the origins of the American Indians. Fantastic and diverse answers were proposed by the early explorers, missionairies, and settlers. Some thought that the Indians were descended from the Ten Lost Tribes of Israel, others that they were descended from inhabitants of the lost continent of Atlantis. One writer suggested that the Indians had reached North America in another Noah's ark.

A later myth, perpetrated by many historians, focused on the relentless persecution during the past five centuries until only a scattering of these "primitive" people remained to be herded onto reservations. This view fails to chronicle the overt and covert ways in which the Indians successfully coped with the intruders.

All of these myths presented one-sided interpretations that ignored the complexity of European and American events and policies. All left serious questions unanswered. What were the origins of the American Indians? Where did they come from? How and when did they get to the New World? What was their life—their culture—really like?

In the late 1800s, anthropologists and archaeologists in the Smithsonian Institution's newly created Bureau of American Ethnology in Washington,

D.C., began to study scientifically the history and culture of the Indians of North America. They were motivated by an honest belief that the Indians were on the verge of extinction and that along with them would vanish their languages, religious beliefs, technology, myths, and legends. These men and women went out to visit, study, and record data from as many Indian communities as possible before this information was forever lost.

By this time there was a new myth in the national consciousness. American Indians existed as figures in the American past. They had performed a historical mission. They had challenged white settlers who trekked across the continent. Once conquered, however, they were supposed to accept graciously the way of life of their conquerors.

The reality again was different. American Indians resisted both actively and passively. They refused to lose their unique identity, to be assimilated into white society. Many whites viewed the Indians not only as members of a conquered nation but also as "inferior" and "unequal." The rights of the Indians could be expanded, contracted, or modified as the conquerors saw fit. In every generation, white society asked itself what to do with the American Indians. Their answers have resulted in the twists and turns of federal Indian policy.

There were two general approaches. One way was to raise the Indians to a "higher level" by "civilizing" them. Zealous missionaries considered it their Christian duty to elevate the Indian through conversion and scanty education. The other approach was to ignore the Indians until they disappeared under pressure from the ever-expanding white society. The myth of the "vanishing Indian" gave stronger support to the latter option, helping to justify the taking of the Indians' land.

Prior to the end of the 18th century, there was no national policy on Indians simply because the American nation had not yet come into existence. American Indians similarly did not possess a political or social unity with which to confront the various Europeans. They were not homogeneous. Rather, they were loosely formed bands and tribes, speaking nearly 300 languages and thousands of dialects. The collective identity felt by Indians today is a result of their common experiences of defeat and/or mistreatment at the hands of whites.

During the colonial period, the British crown did not have a coordinated policy toward the Indians of North America. Specific tribes (most notably the Iroquois and the Cherokee) became military and political pawns used by both the crown and the individual colonies. The success of the American Revolution brought no immediate change. When the United States acquired new territory from France and Mexico in the early 19th century, the federal government wanted to open this land to settlement by homesteaders. But the Indian tribes that lived on this land had signed treaties with European governments assuring their title to the land. Now the United States assumed legal responsibility for honoring these treaties.

At first, President Thomas Jefferson believed that the Louisiana Purchase contained sufficient land for both the Indians and the white population. Within a generation, though, it became clear that the Indians would not be allowed to remain. In the 1830s the federal government began to coerce the eastern tribes to sign treaties agreeing to relinquish their ancestral land and move west of the Mississippi River. Whenever these negotiations failed, President Andrew Jackson used the military to remove the Indians. The southeastern tribes, promised food and transportation during their removal to the West, were instead forced to walk the "Trail of Tears." More than 4,000 men, woman, and children died during this forced march. The "removal policy" was successful in opening the land to homesteaders, but it created enormous hardships for the Indians.

By 1871 most of the tribes in the United States had signed treaties ceding most or all of their ancestral land in exchange for reservations and welfare. The treaty terms were intended to bind both parties for all time. But in the General Allotment Act of 1887, the federal government changed its policy again. Now the goal was to make tribal members into individual landowners and farmers, encouraging their absorption into white society. This policy was advantageous to whites who were eager to acquire Indian land, but it proved disastrous for the Indians. One hundred thirty-eight million acres of reservation land were subdivided into tracts of 160, 80, or as little as 40 acres, and allotted tribe members on an individual basis. Land owned in this way was said to have "trust status" and could not be sold. But the surplus land—all Indian land not allotted to individuals—was opened (for sale) to white settlers. Ultimately, more than 90 million acres of land were taken from the Indians by legal and illegal means.

The resulting loss of land was a catastrophe for the Indians. It was necessary to make it illegal for Indians to sell their land to non-Indians. The Indian Reorganization Act of 1934 officially ended the allotment period. Tribes that voted to accept the provisions of this act were reorganized, and an effort was made to purchase land within preexisting reservations to restore an adequate land base.

Ten years later, in 1944, federal Indian policy again shifted. Now the federal government wanted to get out of the "Indian business." In 1953 an act of Congress named specific tribes whose trust status was to be ended "at the earliest possible time." This new law enabled the United States to end unilaterally, whether the Indians wished it or not, the special status that protected the land in Indian tribal reservations. In the 1950s federal Indian policy was to transfer federal responsibility and jurisdiction to state governments, encourage the physical relocation of Indian peoples from reservations to urban areas, and hasten the termination, or extinction, of tribes.

Between 1954 and 1962 Congress passed specific laws authorizing the termination of more than 100 tribal groups. The stated purpose of the termination policy was to ensure the full and complete integration of Indians into American society. However, there is a less benign way to interpret this legislation. Even as termination was being discussed in Congress, 133 separate bills were introduced to permit the transfer of trust land ownership from Indians to non-Indians.

With the Johnson administration in the 1960s the federal government began to reject termination. In the 1970s yet another Indian policy emerged. Known as "self-determination," it favored keeping the protective role of the federal government while increasing tribal participation in, and control of, important areas of local government. In 1983 President Reagan, in a policy statement on Indian affairs, restated the unique "government is government" relationship of the United States with the Indians. However, federal programs since then have moved toward transferring Indian affairs to individual states, which have long desired to gain control of Indian land and resources.

As long as American Indians retain power, land, and resources that are coveted by the states and the federal government, there will continue to be a "clash of cultures," and the issues will be contested in the courts, Congress, the White House, and even in the international human rights community. To give all Americans a greater comprehension of the issues and conflicts involving American Indians today is a major goal of this series. These issues are not easily understood, nor can these conflicts be readily resolved. The study of North American Indian history and culture is a necessary and important step toward that comprehension. All Americans must learn the history of the relations between the Indians and the federal government, recognize the unique legal status of the Indians, and understand the heritage and cultures of the Indians of North America.

Slow Bull, an Oglala Lakota religious leader. Native American religious leaders usually obtain their status through their knowledge and command of spirit power.

SPIRIT POWERS

Religion—the belief in the supernatural—has influenced lives and affected culture throughout human history. Different religions may bear little or no superficial resemblance to each other, but all religions serve similar purposes. Religious tenets help people make sense of the universe, rendering the random and sometimes threatening events of life into a comprehensible (and perhaps controllable) order. In addition, religious dogma often provides people with a guide to behavior, giving them a moral and ethical framework in which to make decisions. Religion holds together communities as well, uniting people of a specific faith to perform rituals that celebrate their common identity.

There is no one single Native American religion. Of the hundreds of different Native American tribes in North America, most have their own unique set of religious beliefs, and some have two or three competing dogmas. Despite this variety, certain commonalities can be found in Native American religious beliefs and practices. One frequently held belief is that supernatural beings and forces actively and regularly affect human lives, protecting people from danger, giving people knowledge and understanding of the world, and curing illness. Spirit beings and forces may also harm people who fail to respect their powers by causing disease, death, and other misfortunes. Practitioners of these religions try to learn as much as possible about the spirit world in order to determine what type of behavior will please its inhabitants. These people seek ways of forming direct contact with the supernatural realm so that they can acquire spiritual knowledge, powers, and protection for themselves and their families.

In the view of many Native Americans, the natural and supernatural worlds are inseparable because people's lives are affected by events in both realms. Just as humans interact with animals, plants, and other humans in their day-to-day lives, they regularly interact with spirit beings and forces. The natural and supernatural worlds are tied together by spirit power, an idea that is fundamental to all Native American religions, although it varies in detail among different peoples.

Spirit power is the source of knowledge and abilities. It affects the events in a person's life and can be used to control their outcome. While this power is wielded by supernatural beings, it does not exist only in the supernatural realm. Spirit power is often thought to be a spiritual essence that resides in all living beings, all forms and forces of nature, and all material objects—a kind of cosmic energy. Although everything contains power, power exists apart from the objects that it inhabits. As stated by Francis LaFlesche, an Osage of the midwestern plains,

> All life is *wakan* [power]. So also is everything which exhibits power, whether in action, as the winds and drifting clouds, or in passive endurance, as the boulder by the wayside. For even the commonest sticks and stones have a spiritual essence which must be reverenced as a manifestation of the all-pervading mysterious power that fills the universe.

The Lakotas (Sioux) of the northern Great Plains have a similar concept of spiritual essence, also called wakan. To the Oglala Lakota spiritual leader, Sword,

> *Wakan* means very many things. The Lakota understands what it means from the things that are considered *wakan*. . . . When a priest uses any object in performing a ceremony that object becomes endowed with a spirit, not exactly a spirit, but something like one, the priests call it *tonwan* or *ton*. Now anything that acquires *ton* is *wakan*, because it is the power of the spirit or quality that has been put into it. . . .
>
> *Wakan* comes from the *wakan* beings. These *wakan* beings are greater than mankind in the same way that mankind is greater than animals. They are never born and never die. They can do many things that mankind cannot do. Mankind can pray to the *wakan* beings for help.

In the belief system of the Kwakiutls (kwa-key-YOU-tils) of British Columbia, spirit power is an invisible force that is found in all beings and objects. Although the power is invisible, it can if it wishes take on various external shapes. To the Kwakiutls, spirit power is constantly in motion, constantly changing into and out of different visible forms. Consequently, while the outward appearance of an entity is temporary, its inner spiritual essence is eternal. Power is contained in many objects, including ritual paraphernalia such as sacred costumes and masks that are worn by the Kwakiutls when conducting ceremonies. These costumes and masks are not merely adornments but are themselves spiritual objects, and when ritualists wear this spirit clothing, they can use

A Kwakiutl raven mask that opens to reveal a representation of a deity known as Raven of the Sea. Such masks are often considered spiritually powerful and are closely associated with the deity they represent.

the power contained within it to benefit humans.

The Ojibwas of eastern and central Canada believe that power, called *manitou,* is an all-pervasive force that is embodied in supernatural beings and sacred objects. Indeed, sacred objects are sanctified by virtue of the manitou contained in them. Like the Kwakiutls, the Ojibwas believe that spirit beings and forces are constantly in motion and can change their shapes, becoming visible as animals, humans, or material objects. Objects that are inhabited by spirit power are alive and sentient, and they can be used by humans as sources of power for beneficial activities (such as curing illness and providing protection) or for harmful activities (such as causing disease and misfortune). In the Ojibwa religion, the power itself is neutral; only its application is good or evil.

Since the Ojibwas believe that power is constantly changing its shape, it is not always possible to know whether any particular object contains power. An Ojibwa man, when asked by researcher A. Irving Hallowell whether all stones are alive, answered "No! But *some* are." The only way to discover if an object has power is to observe and test it carefully—for example, if a stone behaves like a living being, it is alive and contains power. The Ojibwa man interviewed by Hallowell reported that his father had once performed a ritual cure using a large round stone. At the beginning of the healing ceremony, the father walked twice around the stone and then started to sing. According to the man interviewed, the stone began "following the trail of the old man around the tent, rolling over and over, I saw it happen several times and others saw it too." The stone had demonstrated by its actions that it had power and was alive. Since the stone was (literally) powerful, the man's father could tap its power and use it in a healing ritual.

The powers of beings, forces, and objects are sometimes revealed to people through visionary experiences. The Hurons of Ontario and the Iroquois (Irro-kwoys) of New York, Ontario, and Quebec believe that spirit power often comes to people in dreams. Power appears in the form of spirit beings who speak to dreamers, giving instructions or solutions for specific problems and transmitting messages from the dead. In addition, they give dreamers prayers and songs to recite when in danger or need. Through visions and dreams, a lifelong personal bond is established between an individual and a specific source of spiritual power.

To the Western Apaches of Arizona, spirit power is an intangible essence that exists in many forms and forces of nature, especially in water, fire, thunder, rain, lightning, wind, the moon, and the sun. Supernatural deities and sacred medicines also have spirit power. Although humans do not have spirit power as part of their nature, they can obtain it in several ways. People acquire power by praying for spiritual knowledge and learning the songs and rituals needed to properly utilize power. In some cases, powers reveal themselves to people spontaneously. A Western Apache man living in Cibecue, Arizona, once recounted:

> Over there at Gleason Flat, one time, I was working cattle. That day was sure hot. Then, just when I was looking in that brush country for some cow, it started to rain. Sure rain hard. So I went with my horse under a tree. Right then some lightning hit [approximately 20 yards away] and start rolling at me. I was sure scared. But then that lightning stopped and went into the ground just when it got to me. Then, another lightning did just like that. Come at me and go into the ground. After that I thought about it. When I got back to Cibecue,

An Apache man, outfitted with a mask, headdress, body paint, and costume, performs a dance. Such elaborate costumes are often believed to give the dancer special powers.

> I started learning songs. I knew that power wanted me to use it.

Acquiring and learning to use spirit power is a deeply emotional ordeal. Even when the ability to manipulate spirit power is actively sought, the experience can be frightening because the power itself is dangerous. Since power comes from the world of spirits, not the world of humans, people can never fully control it. Humans may have access to power, but it acts on its own even when it is operating through a human agent. Sanapia, a Comanche healer from Oklahoma, recalled a dramatic episode in her training as a healer when her mother picked up some live coals from a fire, gave them to her, and told her to rub them over her hands. Sanapia was surprised to find that the hot coals did not burn her:

> I was sure scared then . . . almost got up and ran away. I was only a young girl at that time, you know. But, when I took them coals on my hand, inside and outside my hand I felt a chill, maybe. Oh, it was like chills in my hands. That has the meaning that power was in there . . . working in my hands. Felt like it would go up my arm even.

A Navajo mask, made of painted hide, cotton cloth, shells, and wood, that was used in healing rites.

Many Native American religions teach that the cosmic energy of spirit power is released through prayers and songs. To the Navajos of Arizona and New Mexico, the voice itself is powerful since it is thought to be akin to wind, the strongest cosmic force. Among some Native American peoples of the Southwest, including the Hopis and Zunis, sacred words must be recited exactly as passed down through religious tradition. If a person omits anything or makes a mistake in the order of lines, the prayer or ritual will be ineffective. In other societies, spontaneous prayers and songs are seen as divinely inspired. Orpingalik, an Inuit (IN-nu-it) man of the Canadian Arctic, told the Danish researcher Knud Rasmussen that

> Songs are thoughts, sung out with the breath when people are moved by great forces and ordinary speech no longer suffices.
>
> Man is moved just like the ice floe sailing here and there out in the current. His thoughts are driven by a flowing force when he feels joy, when he feels fear, when he feels sorrow. Thoughts can wash over him like a flood, making his breath come in gasps and his heart throb. . . . And then it will happen that we, who always think we are small, will feel still smaller. And we will fear to use words. But it will happen that the words we need will come of themselves. When the words we want to use shoot up of themselves—we get a new song.

Dance is an especially important feature of Native American religious ceremonies. Participants in sacred dances not only express their respect for spirit beings but are also vehicles for transmitting spirit power to their communities. By dressing in costumes and masks, dancers from such diverse cultures as the Kwakiutls, Iroquois, Zunis, and Navajos actually embody spirit forces. The sacred costumes and masks transform the dancers into the beings they represent.

The supernatural beings, sacred objects, and the means of worship and veneration found in many traditional Native American religious ceremonies express each culture's underlying beliefs about the nature of the universe. Such beliefs are also expressed through stories, legends, and myths, especially creation stories, which describe the history of the universe, map out its current shape, and explain how and why the universe became what it is today. ▲

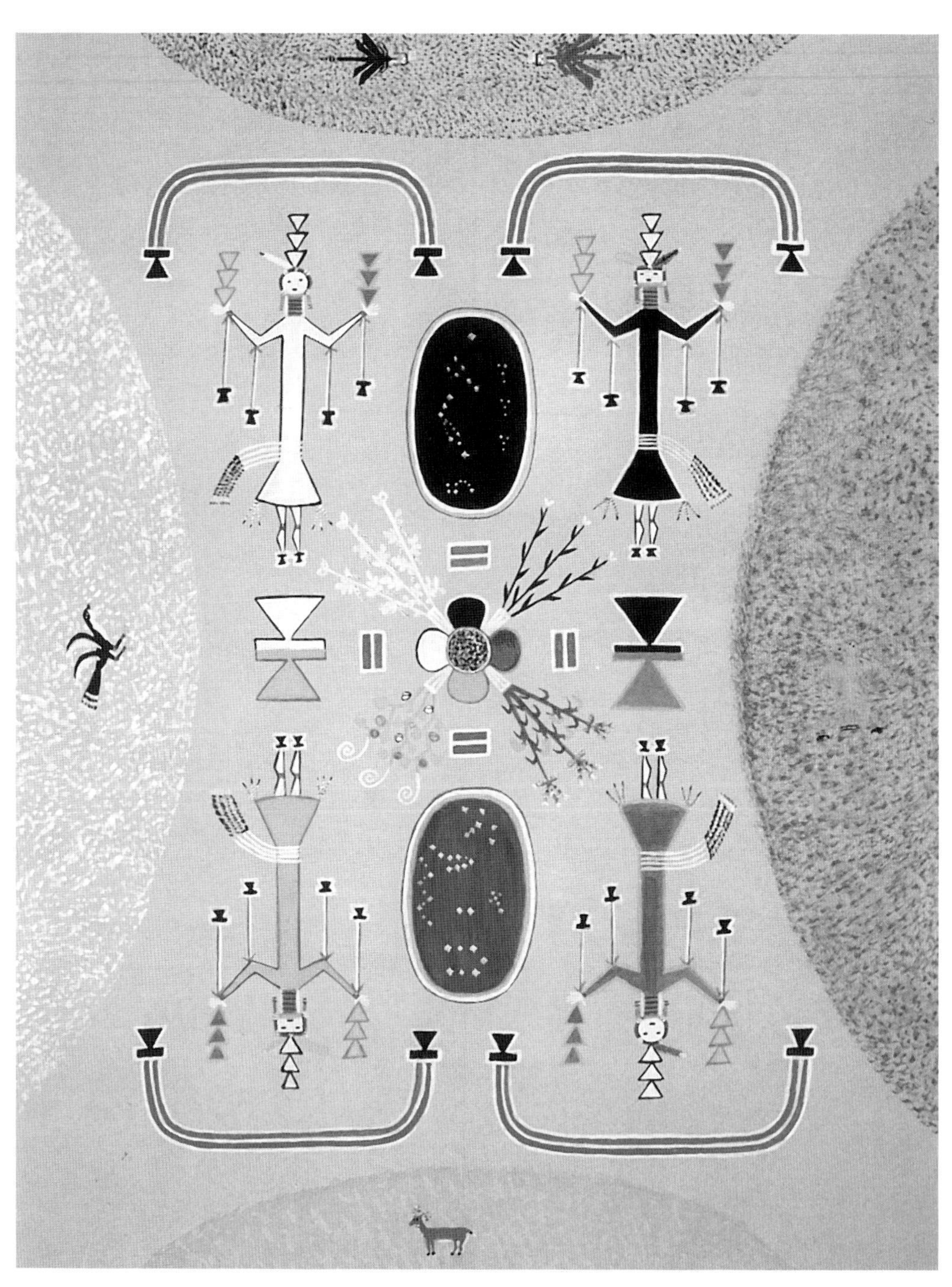

A Navajo sandpainting shows the four protective supernatural beings who lie on the horizon between the cardinal directions of east, south, west, and north.

IN THE BEGINNING

In most Native American mythologies, the universe has always existed, although its present appearance may be different from its original state. Consequently, stories of creation do not usually recount any absolute beginnings but rather deal with the transformation of a primeval universe into the present-day world. These myths often focus on the supernatural creators or transformers who played an important part in changing the world and creating the conditions in which human beings now live. In addition, they transmit ideas about the current shape of the universe, including the placement of the earth, waters, sky, and air.

Stories of creation do more than describe the origins and inhabitants of the world. By recounting the process of transforming the world, these stories teach people about the relationships that exist among all living things. They also convey philosophical attitudes and provide moral lessons that help people understand and cope with events in their lives. The underlying lessons of these stories are often considered far more important than the details of the tale itself—a priority expressed by one Zuni man, who, while reciting a legend to an anthropologist who was carefully recording every word, interrupted himself to demand, "When I tell you these stories, do you *see* it, or do you just write it down?"

The Navajo creation myth states that the universe consists of a number of worlds that each have the shape of a round disk or platter. These disklike worlds are stacked on top of one another and are connected by colored columns. Navajos believe that we are now living in the fifth world. There are four worlds beneath our own and several that exist above, although the exact number is not certain. Life began in the first, or bottommost, world, where people initially lived in peace and happiness. But conditions in the first world soon deteriorated through a series of disasters and misfortunes. Floods, diseases, and conflicts became widespread, and to escape these calamities people fled to the next world. There they lived happily for a short while, but, as before, conflict and misery arose, causing people to once again flee to the next world. The third and fourth worlds were likewise initially comfortable, but they too became inhospitable because of renewed misfortunes. In each of the four worlds, calamities were caused by people's inability to control their desires and behavior. For example, adultery caused many disasters, and incidents of incest led to the creation of disease as well as the rise of evil witchcraft.

After a long time, people emerged into the fifth and current world. At the edges of the fifth world are four sacred mountains, identified today as Mount Taylor, Sierra Blanca Peak, San Francisco Peaks, and Mount Hesperus. The edges of the world are protected by four supernatural beings, who lie on the horizon between the cardinal directions of east, south, west, and north. Dawn Man lies on the horizon from east to south, Horizontal Blue Man lies from south to west, Evening Twilight Woman lies from west to north, and Darkness Woman lies from north to east.

Within this world guarded by deities, the people now live. They try to abide by principles of harmony in order to maintain happiness and peace. These ideals are expressed by the Navajo word *hozho,* which is usually translated into English as *beauty* but has a meaning that is much more complex than the English word. Hozho means all that is good, favorable, desirable, beautiful, pleasant, peaceful, and harmonious; in addition, the word refers both to these qualities and to the conditions in which they exist. Many Navajo prayers relate the people's desire for this type of beauty. For example, one prayer says:

In beauty may we dwell.
In beauty may we walk.
In beauty may our male kindred dwell.
In beauty may our female kindred dwell.
In beauty may it rain on us.
In beauty may our corn grow.
In beauty all around us may it rain.
In beauty may we walk.
The beauty is restored.

The Navajo story of people's emergence into the current world transmits important cultural messages, emphasizing both the positive effects of maintaining valued behavior and the negative results of violating social norms. The problems that people had to endure in the four previous worlds were caused by the people themselves when they could not control disruptive and excessive behavior. They quarreled, plotted against one another, and acted purely out of lust and greed. Because of their conduct, they were unable to sustain harmonious relations with one another and with the world, and disaster befell them. In order to maintain a livable, peaceful world, the Navajos believe, the evil inherent in people must be controlled.

The Iroquois have a different creation myth that also emphasizes important cultural values and beliefs. They say that before the present-day earth was formed, all that existed was sky above and water below. In the Sky-World lived a woman called Sky-Woman who was pregnant. One day, she went out to find herbal medicines for her husband. As she dug near the roots of a large tree, a hole opened up around the roots, and Sky-Woman fell toward the waters below. She feared that she would die, but the birds and the animals in the waters saw her falling and decided to save her life. Several birds flew up to Sky-Woman and supported her with their outspread wings, easing her fall. Muskrat quickly dove beneath the water and brought up a handful of soft mud to place on the back of Snapping Turtle, and Sky-Woman landed unharmed on Turtle's back. The mud that Muskrat had placed there gradually expanded to become the earth, and the world now rests on the back of the first giant Turtle.

Sky-Woman soon gave birth to a daughter. When the daughter grew up, she became pregnant and gave birth to twin sons. One son, called Sapling, was born in the normal manner, but the second boy, named Flint, exited his mother's body through her armpit, killing her in the process. Sky-Woman buried her daughter in the earth, and from her body grew corn, beans, and squash. Since that time, these plants, called Our Life Supporters by the Iroquois, have been an essential source of sustenance for humans.

The twin boys proceeded to create many of the animals and plants that exist in the world, but they hated each other and were always trying to outdo one another. Sapling created good plants such as berries and fruits, so Flint made briers and poison ivy. As their competition increased, Flint tried to spoil Sapling's creations. When Sapling made fish in the rivers and lakes, Flint put many small bones in their bodies to choke the people who ate them. When Sapling made rivers and streams flow in both directions so that people could easily travel wherever they wanted to go, Flint changed the course of water so that the rivers flowed only in one direction, making it difficult for people to travel upstream.

Sapling and Flint constantly challenged each other. In one contest, the two competed to see who could best move a mountain. Flint tried first and failed, but when Sapling tried his strength, he moved the mountain easily. As Flint turned around to see what was happening, his face hit against the mountain, smashing his nose and making it bent and twisted. The twins also fought constantly. After many battles, Sapling managed to get Flint at a disadvantage. Just as Sapling was about to kill Flint, he offered to spare his brother if he would use his powers to cure the illnesses that he had originated. Flint agreed, and he has since been the spirit source of healing medicines.

The Iroquois' story of creation and transformation emphasizes two prominent themes that recur in their religion

Creations Battle *by Mohawk artist John Fadden dramatizes the battle between the twin deities Flint and Sapling for dominance during the creation of the world.*

and philosophy. The story stresses the importance of women's fertility and their role in the continuation of life. In the primordial world, women were not only the procreators of new life through the ordinary process of birth, but they also created the plants that are basic to the Iroquois' diet. The second theme that emerges is that the forces of good and evil need to be balanced. Sapling represents the good, beneficial, and positive aspects of the world and society, while Flint represents the bad, malevolent, and negative aspects of life. Sapling's decision not to kill Flint when he had the opportunity is similar to humanity's inability to totally eliminate evil. But Sapling did not simply let Flint go; he first obtained Flint's promise to use his considerable powers to help people. This bargain expresses people's need to control and transform the evil forces both in themselves and in the world around them. But unlike Sapling, humans do not have enough power to control evil on their own; they must rely on the aid of spirits, which can be obtained through prayers and rituals.

The Zunis of New Mexico have yet another view of creation. In the beginning, they say, a deity named Awonawilona lived alone in the universe. Nothing else existed, and space was filled with fog and steam. Then Awonawilona, a being both male and female, created the clouds and waters from its breath and later formed the rest of the universe. This universe consists of nine layers. The earth, which occupies the middle level, is a large circular island surrounded by oceans. Lakes, rivers, and springs on the earth are connected to the oceans by underground linkages. The sky is an upside-down bowl of stone, resting above the earth. Each of the other eight layers of the universe are home to different kinds of animals, birds, and trees.

At first, people lived under the earth's surface in the fourth and innermost layer of the universe, deep inside the body of Earth Mother. These people did not look like humans do today. Their bodies were covered with slime, they had webbed hands and feet, and they had tails. They did not realize how strange they looked because they could not see clearly in the darkness of the earth. After a while, Sun Father decided to bring people out of the earth because he was lonely. Sun Father told his twin sons, the War Gods, to lead the Zunis outside. The War Gods helped the people climb up a ladder from inside the earth and then changed the people's appearance, removing the slime from their bodies and making their hands and feet normal.

The Zunis remained near their place of emergence for a time. Then deities told them to go forth and find the middle place, or *itiwana,* of the universe, where they should build their villages. Prominent Zuni religious leaders called Rain Priests led the people on a journey that took many years. Each time they chose a place to settle, some misfortune occurred that forced them to move again. Each time, the Zunis understood that they had not yet found the itiwana of the world.

A guard watches at the entrance to the Antelope kiva in the Hopi village of Walpi. Like the Zunis, the Hopis believe that their ancestors originally lived deep inside the earth; this kiva contains a special pit inside that symbolizes the place of their emergence to the outer world.

At last, the Zunis met an old man who was a powerful Rain Priest. When one of the Zunis' own Rain Priests prayed with the old man, a heavy rainstorm fell. Suddenly, a giant water spider came by, spread out its six legs, and told the people that the itiwana was directly under its heart. The Zunis knew its message to be true. They set about building their villages, constructing one at the itiwana and six others at locations marked off by the spider's six legs. Once their villages were established, the Zunis erected an altar at the exact site of the itiwana. On the altar, they placed sacred objects belonging to the Rain Priests, which became reminders of the people's journey and of their duty to honor the powerful deities who led them there. The altar remains today at the center of the village of Zuni. On it rests a stone that contains the eternal beating heart of the itiwana of the world.

The Zunis' story of creation and emergence situates their people in the center of the world. But for the Zunis, the itiwana is not merely a geographical center but is also a spiritual and philosophical base. This center represents balance, harmony, stability, and the solid, fundamental core of human experience. The center is the merging of all time, all space, and all existence. The creation story also reveals the people's reliance on the knowledge and powers derived from spirits. The supernatural twin War Gods not only led the people out of the earth but gave the people the shape and appearance they have today. In addition, the instructions and messages from the deities caused the Zunis to both seek and find the itiwana, where they could make their home.

The Snohomishs (snow-HO-mishes) of Washington State have a different creation myth, wherein the world was created by a deity named Changer. Changer began making the world in the East and slowly traveled westward, creating the mountains, rivers, and lakes as

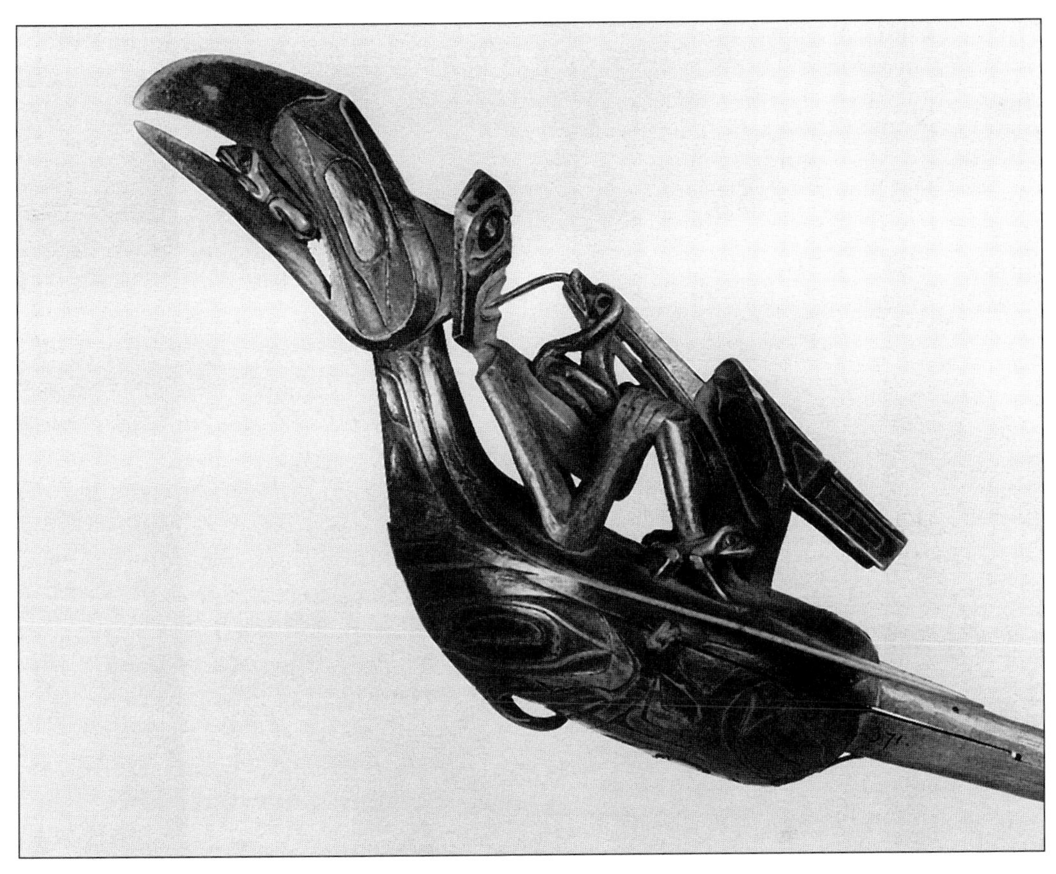

A carved wooden Kwakiutl rattle portrays a raven carrying a man on his back who has frogs on his chest and on his feet. Cooperation and interaction between animals and humans are common themes in Native American mythology.

he walked. He made all of the plants, birds, and animals that live on earth. And he made people, giving each group a different language. When Changer arrived at Puget Sound in present-day Washington State, he decided to go no farther because the land and sea were so beautiful. But he had many languages left over so he threw them up in the air, scattering them all around the region. This is why there are so many different languages spoken by the tribes of the Northwest.

When the humans saw how Changer had made the world, they were not pleased—Changer had made the sky so low that tall people bumped their heads against it. After a time, leaders of all the different groups of people met and devised a plan to lift the sky. "We can do it,'' said a wise man, ''if we all push at the same time. We will need all the people and all the animals and all the birds when we push.'' But one of the leaders asked: ''How will we know when to push? Some of us live in this part of the world, some in another. We don't all talk the same language. How can we get everyone to push at the same time?'' The leaders decided on a signal that someone would shout when they were all ready. The people, animals, and birds then made long poles from giant fir trees. They lifted the poles to touch the sky. The signal was given and everybody raised their poles, slowly pushing up the sky.

This creation story not only transmits the Snohomishs' beliefs about the origin of the universe and its inhabitants but also conveys a moral message about the need for cooperation among all living things—even among members of different nations or species. This story also emphasizes the power of people to make changes in the basic order of the universe. Changer is not a perfect god whose decisions cannot be challenged; he is a fallible if powerful deity whose admittedly beneficial actions sometimes need correction. Since actions made in the supernatural realm affect humans, humans cannot ignore supernatural goings-on but must stay involved in such matters in order to maintain a pleasant and livable world.

Besides emphasizing certain cultural values and explaining natural phenomena, creation stories help explain the roles of the various supernatural beings in each tribe's mythology. The roles of these beings vary widely—some have specific powers or duties in their relations with humans, while others are more distant. But all deities can cause hardship if displeased; in addition, malevolent monsters, dwarfs, giants, and other dangerous supernatural creatures can harm people. Creation myths provide all these powerful supernatural creatures with a background and history, enabling people to better understand how best to please (or to avoid) them.

By no means are all Native American myths creation myths. Many myths detail the exploits of superhuman figures who lived in ancient times. These adventures teach moral lessons and demonstrate both the rewards given for brave and proper actions and the punishments meted out to wrongdoers. Other Native American legends tell of the adventures of special characters, usually animals or birds, called tricksters. Tricksters have great powers that they can use for both good and evil. In some legends, they are the creators or transformers of mountains, lakes, celestial bodies, animals, plants, or humans, and they may also be responsible for the origination of illness and death. But these creations are usually an unintended side effect of the trickster's exploits because tricksters are almost always entirely self-centered and wish simply to pursue their own desires to the limit, regardless of the consequences. They often suffer for their selfish behavior, yet they manage to survive. Stories

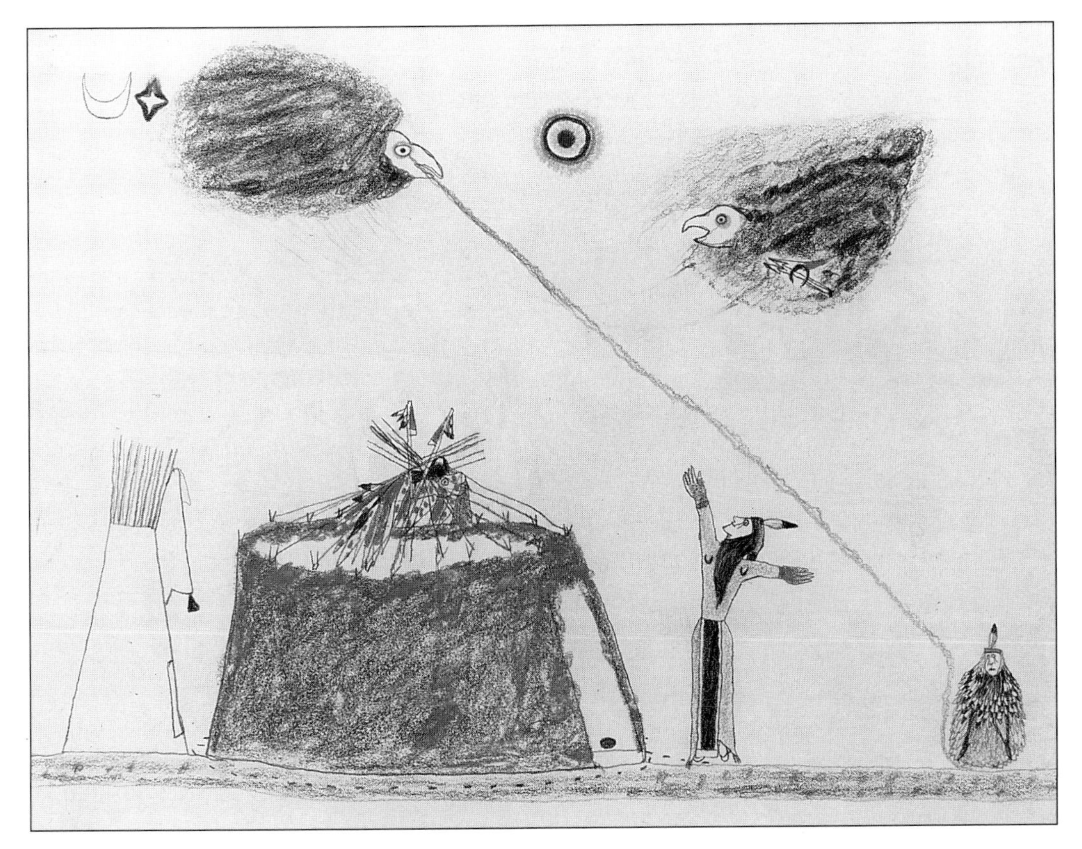

This drawing, made around 1875 by Kiowa artist Wohaw, shows a man engaging in a Sun Dance ritual while powerful supernatural creatures called Thunderbirds fly overhead and shoot power into a mysterious figure. Many Native American legends explain the origin and behavior of such supernatural beings.

about tricksters transmit moral teachings, express cultural attitudes, and of course entertain narrators and listeners alike.

The Blackfeet of the western Great Plains tell of a tricksters' race between Old Man and Coyote. One day, Old Man saw some deer and elk playing a game of follow the leader. Old Man joined the game, sang a song, and, as the leader, led the animals to the edge of a cliff. Old Man jumped down and was knocked senseless. When he recovered, he called to the elk to follow his lead. The animals hesitated because they were afraid of being hurt, but Old Man said "Oh! It's nice and soft here. Jump now!" The elk jumped down and were killed by the fall. Then Old Man called to the deer to jump down. The deer said, "No, we shall

Four real-life tricksters, clowns from the San Juan Pueblo in New Mexico, make faces and mock people in this 1940 photograph. Like the legendary trickster figures, Pueblo clowns often embody negative personality traits.

not jump down, because the elk are all killed," but Old Man insisted that the elk were only playacting. The deer jumped down and were also killed. Old Man butchered the animals and carried the meat back to his camp.

Soon Coyote came by, wearing a shell around his neck. One of his legs was tied up as though it were badly hurt. Coyote asked Old Man for something to eat. Old Man offered to give Coyote meat in exchange for his shell, but Coyote refused because the shell was his protective medicine. Then Old Man noticed that Coyote's leg was bandaged and said, "Well, I'll run you a race for a meal." Coyote answered, "I am hurt. I cannot run." But Old Man insisted that they run a long race out to a point far distant from his camp and back again, and Coyote finally agreed. On the way out from the camp, Coyote ran very slowly, crying for Old Man to wait for him, but when the two reached the turning point, clever Coyote suddenly tore the bandage off his leg and sped back to camp, leaving Old Man far behind. Coyote called to all the coyotes and mice and other animals, telling them to come to Old Man's camp for a good meal, and they feasted on Old Man's kill. Old Man ran and ran, trying to get back to his camp before all his food was gone, calling out pitifully all the while, "Leave me some meat, leave me some meat."

Both the humanlike Old Man and the animal-like Coyote act as tricksters in this story, a fact that neatly underlines a point made by folklorist Stith Thompson regarding Native American trickster figures: "Usually it is quite impossible to tell whether animal or person is in the mind of the narrator. The distinction is never very clear." Indeed, for many years folklorists debated whether a character like Coyote was supposed to be an animal with human characteristics or a human with an animal name. More recent scholarship has suggested, however, that at least among certain tribes a character like Coyote would get his name not because of his actual species, but because of his personality. As in many societies, Native Americans often associate certain animals with specific human personality traits. (Familiar examples in contemporary American culture are the association of dogs with loyalty, foxes with cleverness, and mules with stubbornness.) A character who embodies or exaggerates a certain trait—and trickster figures usually personify negative traits, such as boastfulness, stinginess, greed, belligerence, cruelty, lewdness, and spitefulness—may receive the name of the animal that is believed to best represent this trait. Consequently, in some Native American languages, trickster figures are not given the name of a single animal but instead are named generically after the species. In such languages, the name Coyote would be better translated as "coyotes in general" or even "coyoteness," reflecting the fact that the character Coyote embodies certain personality traits considered characteristic of coyotes.

The lack of distinction between animal and human protagonists in Native American myths can be found elsewhere in Native American religious beliefs. Although animals are generally considered different from people, they do have spiritual power (as do plants and natural forces) which makes for a sort of supernatural equivalence among the things of the world. This perceived equivalence has resulted in a multitude of beliefs and ceremonies focused on the natural world and its nonhuman inhabitants. ▲

SMYRNA PUBLIC LIBRARY

A Native American whaler prepares his gear. The importance of whaling and other forms of hunting is reflected in the many ceremonies that surround such activities.

RENEWING THE EARTH

All people depend on animals and plants for food. In order to live, humans must eat. In order to eat, humans must kill animals or harvest plants—in effect sacrificing the lives and the well-being of other species to continue their own. In modern American society, most people are far removed from this process and simply purchase food at stores and restaurants with little thought of how it got there, where it came from, or what would happen if it were no longer available. In traditional Native American societies, however, people are quite aware of their reliance on other species. Since a central tenet of most Native American religions is that all living creatures should show respect for one another, many public and private religious activities are centered on maintaining harmonious relationships between humans and the other living things on which they depend. Numerous prayers and rituals exist to honor and thank the spirits of the animals and plants that have died so that people may live.

In many Native American cultures, people pay homage to animals by thanking the animals' spirit protectors. For example, among the Algonquian (al-GONG-kwey-an) tribes of eastern and central Canada, killing a bear requires special rituals. The hunters address the dead bear's spirit with words generally used for kinspeople, dress the bear in ceremonial clothing, and erect a wooden pole nearby on which they hang the bear's skull and offerings of tobacco. After the bear is butchered, its bones are placed on a raised platform so that dogs and other scavengers will not disturb them.

The spirits of bears are believed to appreciate these signs of respect and respond to the honors by allowing more bears to be caught. As a man from one Algonquian tribe, the Saulteaux, explained:

> The bears have a chief, and the orders of this chief must be obeyed. Sometimes he orders a bear to go to

> an Indian trap. When offerings or prayers are made to the chief of the bears, he sends more of his children to the Indians. If this were not done, the spirit of the bear would be offended and would report the circumstances to the chief of bears who would prevent the careless Indians from catching more.

Among the Inuits of the Alaskan and Canadian Arctic, hunting is surrounded by elaborate rituals. For example, the rituals pertaining to the Inuits' whale hunts in northern Alaska begin months before the start of the spring whaling season. A whaling leader, called an *umialik,* recruits a whaling crew and gives each hunter a new set of clothing made by his wife. Many ritual rules and taboos are observed during the days before the men depart on their expeditions. They clean their boat and hunting gear, refrain from eating meat, abstain from sexual activity, and pray to spirits for protection. When the hunting party brings the first whale to shore, the umialik's wife performs a ritual honoring the whale. She dresses in her finest clothing, thanks the whale for allowing itself to be caught, and places a drink of cold water in its mouth.

Native Americans show respect not only to animals but to trees, plants, and earth as well. A member of the Fox tribe, which formerly resided along the banks of the upper Mississippi River, explained:

> We do not like to harm the trees. Whenever we can, we always make an offering of tobacco to the trees before we cut them down. We never waste the wood, but use all that we cut down. If we did not think of their feelings, and did not offer them tobacco before cutting them down, all the other trees in the forest would weep, and that would make our hearts sad, too.

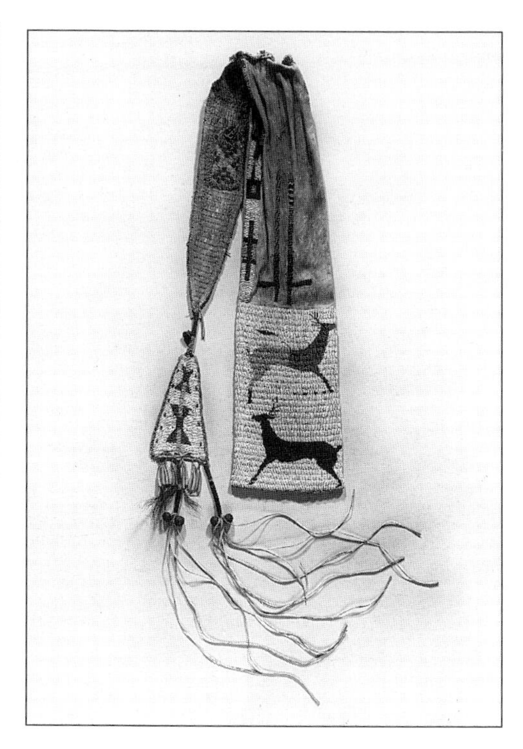

A Lakota pipe bag made to hold a pipe, tobacco, and other smoking implements. The use of the sacred pipe was reportedly taught to the Lakotas by a deity named White Buffalo Calf Woman.

And when Papago women, who live in southern Arizona, dig up clay to make their pots, they offer a prayer of explana-

Miracle, a white buffalo calf, sits with her mother. Born on a Wisconsin farm about 100 miles northwest of Chicago, Illinois, on August 31, 1994, Miracle is the first white female buffalo born in over a century. Since her birth, thousands of devout Native Americans have made pilgrimages to view and to honor her.

tion: "I take only what I need. It is to cook for my children."

In some Native American societies, humanity's dependence on nature is dramatized by myths that claim that certain plant or animal species originated as special gifts given to humans by supernatural beings. For example, the Inuits believe that seals, walrus, and whales originated from the fingers of a deity named Sedna. Sedna was a young woman who lived alone with her father. Several young men asked her to marry, but she refused them all because she did not think them worthy. One day, a handsome young stranger came and proposed marriage, promising to take her to his land far away where she would be honored and lead an easy life. Sedna was enchanted by his promises and went away with him, but she soon discovered that all his words were false. His island home was cold and miserable, and to make matters worse, he was not even human but was in fact a giant bird. Sedna kept crying out in her anguish until one day her father heard his daughter wailing, came across the seas in a boat, and rescued her.

As the two were returning to the mainland, Sedna's husband spotted them. He and his bird compatriots flew over the boat and flapped their huge wings, causing high waves in the sea that threatened to capsize the boat. Sedna's father threw his daughter overboard in order to save his own life. She clung desperately to the side of the boat, but her father took a knife and cut off her fingers. As the fingers fell into the water, they were transformed into seals, walrus, and whales. Sedna sank to the bottom of the ocean but did not die; instead, she took on supernatural powers and now controls the supply of sea animals. Every year, Inuit religious leaders make a spiritual journey to Sedna, asking her to release enough animals for the people's needs. The leaders plead with Sedna to be generous, and they promise Sedna that their people will behave well and will honor her properly.

Another tribe, the Lakotas, believe that the buffalo were given to humanity by a deity known as the White Buffalo Calf Woman. Long ago, while the people were in a summer encampment, their hunters were unable to find any game. One day, two young hunters who were out on the open plains saw a woman approaching in the distance. She was wearing a white buckskin dress that shone brilliantly in the summer sun, and she did not walk on the ground like a normal woman but rather floated in the air. The woman neared them, and one of the hunters reached out to touch her. Instantly, he was struck by lightning and dissolved into a small pile of bones. The mysterious woman spoke to the other hunter, saying

> Good things I am bringing, something holy to your nation. A message I carry for your people from the buffalo nation. Go back to the camp and tell the people to prepare for my arrival. Let it be made holy for my coming.

Four days later, White Buffalo Calf Woman came to the camp. She taught

(continued on page 45)

SHIRTS OF PROTECTION AND POWER

The Ghost Dance religion of the Plains Indians varied considerably from tribe to tribe in its execution and details. Followers of the Ghost Dance religion among the Arapaho, Lakota, and Cheyenne tribes adopted the practice of wearing sacred shirts, known as ghost shirts, that were generally made of pale hide, cotton muslin, or trade leather, decorated with eagle feathers, and painted with holy symbols. Believers wore their ghost shirts constantly, under their clothing in everyday situations and visible during dances and ceremonies. These shirts were believed to provide their wearers with protection and specifically to make them invulnerable to the weapons—especially the bullets—of their enemies.

The origins of the ghost shirt are unclear. Plains warriors traditionally went bare-chested into battle, but many did wear special war shirts during certain ceremonies, of which the ghost shirt may be a modified version. It may also be derived from endowment robes, white robes decorated with sacred symbols that were worn by Mormons as a sign of their faith. Mormon missionaries were especially active among the Plains Indians at this time, and the wearing of hallowed robes may have been one of the numerous elements of Christianity adopted (in a considerably altered form) by the members of the Ghost Dance faith.

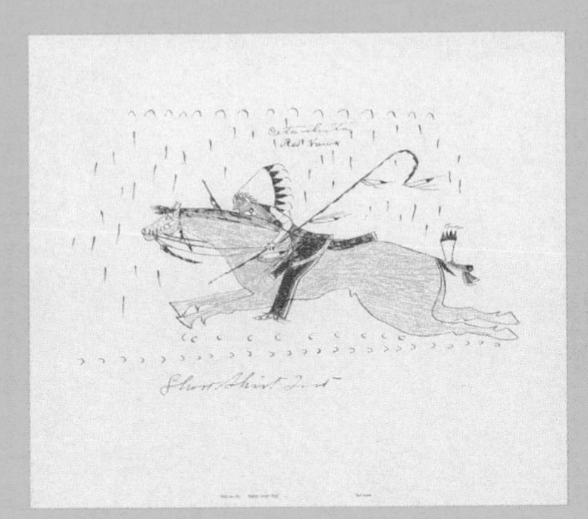

A drawing by Lakota artist Red Hawk shows a warrior testing his ghost shirt against a hail of bullets. This picture and several of the following images were taken from a ledger book found on a Lakota corpse after the massacre at Wounded Knee on January 8, 1891. The ledger drawings have explanatory captions, but the identity and race of the caption-writer remains unknown.

This Arapaho muslin banner, which may have been worn as a cape during Ghost Dance ceremonies, depicts a vision seen by a dance participant. The visionary was led by a man dressed in black silk to stand on the rainbow, from where he could see the earth (small red triangles in the lower right and left corners of the banner), as well as a crow (black bird on rainbow) and an eagle (multicolored bird on rainbow) whose voices (wavy lines) reached the stars.

An unsigned drawing from the Wounded Knee ledger depicts two Lakotas (Sioux) successfully escaping from an enemy thanks to the protection afforded them by their ghost shirts.

An Arapaho woman's dresslike ghost shirt. The figures on the yoke are of a woman flanked by eagles; eagles and a turtle also appear on the skirt. The stars and colors in this dress were probably inspired by the American flag or by U.S. military paraphernalia.

A Lakota warrior charges a group of hostile Crows in this drawing by artist White Magpie. The ghost shirt depicted in this drawing is more of a cape and is made from an untrimmed hide. Although the cape does not actually cover the warrior's front, its magic protects him anyway.

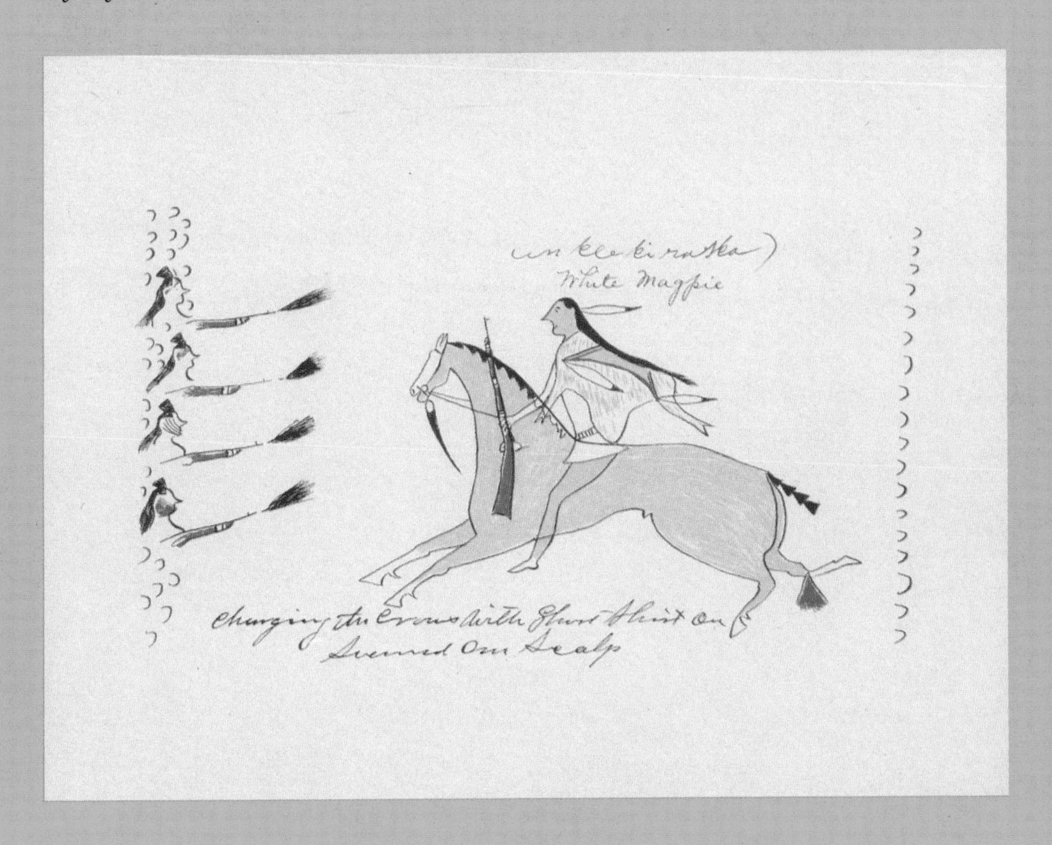

A Lakota ghost shirt from the late 19th century sports a large bird emitting power from its beak and claws. The yoke of small spots around the neck hole represent a shower of harmless bullets. The bird is probably an eagle; eagles were believed to carry a ghost dancer's spirit to the next world whenever the dancer fell into a trance.

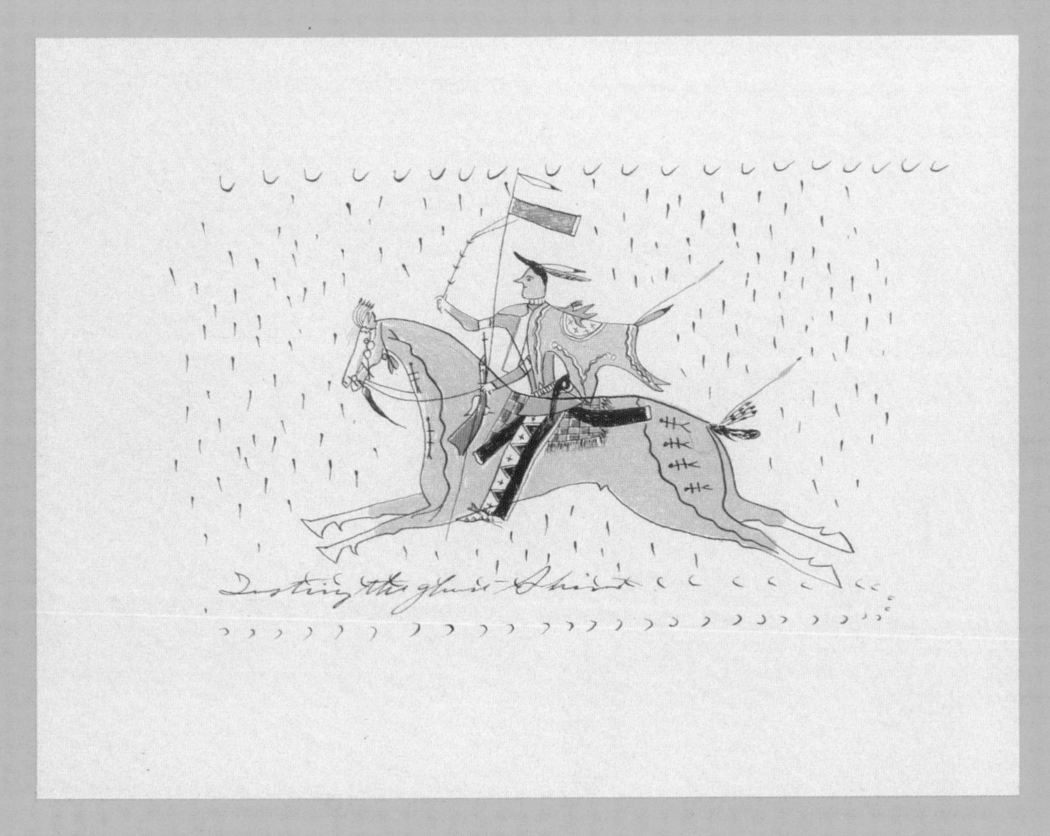

Another unsigned ledger drawing depicts a Lakota warrior wearing a capelike ghost shirt riding unscathed through a test of gunfire. The horse in this drawing has a dragonfly tied to its tail, representing avoidance of danger.

A drawing by Standing Bear shows a Lakota demonstrating the bulletproof nature of his ghost shirt. The caption informs the reader that "Many Indians came to witness this test" of the shirt's power.

(continued from page 36)

the people many prayers and rituals and gave them a sacred pipe to be used in ceremonies, telling them that whenever they smoked it, their messages would be conveyed to the holy spirits. Finally, she left the camp but promised to return again. As she walked off in the distance, she stopped and rolled over four times. In the words of Lame Deer, a Lakota spiritual leader,

> The first time, she turned into a black buffalo; the second into a brown one; the third into a red one; and finally, the fourth time she rolled over, she turned into a white buffalo calf. A white buffalo is the most sacred thing you could ever encounter.

The White Buffalo Calf Woman disappeared over the horizon. As soon as she had vanished, great herds of buffalo appeared and allowed themselves to be killed so that the people might survive. And from that day on, the buffalo furnished the people with everything they needed—meat for their food, skins for their clothes and tipis, bones for their many tools.

Many Native American tribes farmed, and the origins of crops as well as their importance to people were explained through religious stories. Corn was the principal crop of all Native American farmers, and the myths that surround its creation often have special religious significance. The Penobscots of Maine believe that corn originated from the blood of a deity named First Mother. Long ago during a famine, First Mother told her husband to kill her and have her two sons drag her bleeding body across the ground. At first, the man refused, but finally he acceded to her wishes. Wherever First Mother's blood touched the ground, corn grew, and her sacrifice saved the people from starvation.

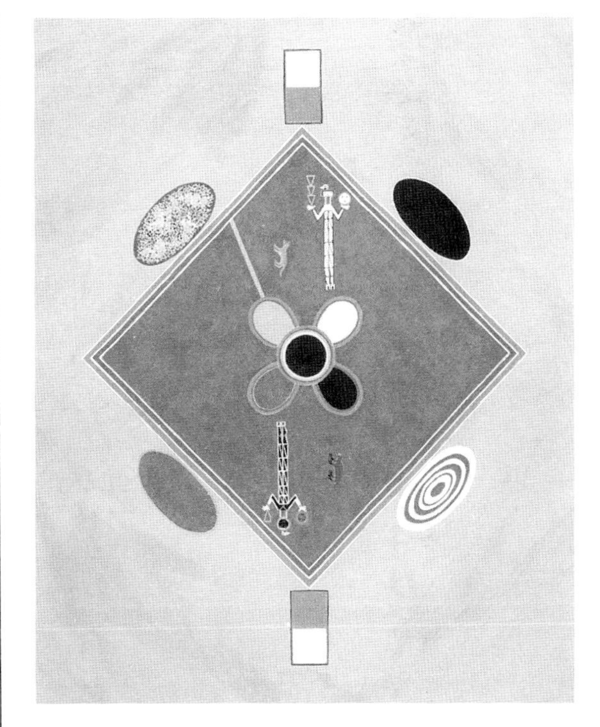

This Navajo sandpainting shows a dark Changing Woman (top), a deity associated with fertility and nature who is credited with giving corn to the tribe.

Many Native American tribes living in eastern North America have similar myths about the origin of corn, wherein the plant grows from a woman's body after her death. Such stories make a metaphoric connection between the fertility of women (which is necessary for the continuance of the tribe) and the fertility of the earth itself. In addition, they reflect a basic tenet of many Native American philosophies, namely that death does not simply follow life but can also lead to and support life.

The farming tribes of the American Southwest also believe that corn was given to people by female deities but do not make the connection between death and corn that is common to the eastern tribes. The Zunis believe that six Corn Maidens brought corn to the people, each giving corn of a different color. According to the Tewas of New Mexico, corn was given by Blue Corn Woman and White Corn Maiden. And the Navajos say that corn originated as a gift from Changing Woman, one of their most beloved deities. Changing Woman, also known as Earth Mother, is associated with all the productive forces of the earth. When she gets old, she changes back to a young woman, mirroring the eternal cycles of growth and decay that the earth itself passes through.

The centrality of corn as a religious symbol for life and fertility is reflected in numerous rituals of the southwestern cultures. The Zunis offer corn or cornmeal to deities as part of nearly every ceremony. For example, when people recite daily prayers to Sun Father at dawn, they sprinkle cornmeal toward the east, the direction of the rising sun. On the eighth day after a baby is born, its paternal grandmother prays for the baby's long life while other female relatives sprinkle cornmeal toward the east. And when a death occurs, the deceased's father's sister rubs cornmeal on the body in order to cleanse and purify it before the soul's journey to the afterworld. The Hopis give a newborn baby two perfect ears of white corn that they call "mothers," and when a Hopi dies, two ears of blue corn are placed in the grave and are believed to accompany the deceased's soul to the afterworld. Corn pollen is a sacred substance to the Navajos. People carry the pollen in small pouches in order to ward off evil forces and maintain health and good fortune, and it is sprinkled on and around patients in most curing rituals. Corn pollen is also associated with women's fertility and is showered on girls during ceremonies marking their puberty.

Weather is also crucial to Native American farmers and gatherers, so many of the religious ceremonies of the Great Plains and the Southwest are focused on bringing rainfall, which is frequently scarce during the growing season. The Lakotas believe that the Thunderers, harbingers of rain, are among the most powerful spirit beings and bring vitality, purity, and long life to those who please them. The majority of Zuni prayers and rituals focus on bringing rain. Indeed, the Zunis have a prestigious religious order called the Rain Priests who make offerings and recite prayers to the supernatural Cloud Beings in order to bring the necessary rain. One such prayer states

> From wherever you abide
> permanently

A Kwakiutl Hamasta initiate, possessed by Cannibal Spirit, dances while clothed in hemlock branches. The initiate must be captured and tamed by the other Hamastas before becoming a member of the society.

You will make your roads come forth
Your little windblown clouds,
Your thin wisps of clouds,
Your great masses of clouds,
Replete with living waters,
You will send forth to stay with us.

Both the Zunis and the Tewas make a complex link between rain and the renewal of life, associating the cycle of human life and death with the cycle of rain and natural growth. They believe that when people die, their souls are eventually transformed into rain clouds. The ancestral spirits return to the tribe as rain clouds, enabling the earth to nurture the crops that the living depend upon for survival.

Native American traditionalists also perform annual ceremonies aimed at renewing the cycle of seasons and restoring harmonious relations among all of earth's creatures and forces. These ceremonies usually occur once a year, marking the end of one cycle of activity and the beginning of the next. They are public rituals that unite all members of a community in a shared experience that both honors the spirits and strengthens the community's bonds.

The Iroquois renewal ceremony, called Midwinter, begins five nights after the first new moon following the winter solstice (December 21). Midwinter is the longest and most complex Iroquois ceremonial, incorporating elements of gratitude, renewal, rejoicing, and preparation for the year ahead. Midwinter lasts nine days, with each day devoted to the performance of a component rite. The first rite of Midwinter (indeed the first rite of all Iroquois ceremonies) is a thanksgiving speech. In the speech, natural and supernatural beings and forces are mentioned and thanked in order, beginning with things close to the earth and proceeding skyward. Terrestrial beings and resources are thanked first, including the people, the earth, waters, plants, trees, animals, birds, and the cultivated foods of corn, beans, and squash. Celestial forms and forces are mentioned next, including wind, thunder, sun, moon, and stars. Finally, thanks are given to supernatural beings. After the recitation of thanksgiving, tobacco is sprinkled on a fire as an invocation to spirits. (The Iroquois, like many other Native Americans, believe that smoke from burning tobacco carries messages to the supernatural realm).

In the next Midwinter rite, two messengers, called Our Uncles, go to each house in the village and announce the order of ceremonies to follow. Our Uncles carry large wooden paddles that they use to stir the ashes in the stove of each household. Ashes from cooking stoves are considered symbols of productivity and health, and the ash-stirring rite represents both community renewal and the awakening of life forces for the coming year.

Originally, during the next Midwinter rite a pure white dog was selected, ritually strangled, and burned. As with tobacco smoke, smoke from burning dogs was believed to carry messages to spirits. Since dogs are loyal to their human owners, the sacrifice of the dog was believed to represent the people's loyalty to supernatural beings. The white dog sacrifice is no longer held today; its place in Midwinter is marked by burning tobacco and reciting sacrificial prayers.

The next several days of Midwinter are devoted to interpreting and fulfilling individual dreams. People go from house to house asking others to guess their dreams based on hints or riddles that the dreamer provides. Each individual gives the dreamer an item that they think might be the one dreamed of. When someone gives the correct object, the dreamer keeps it and returns all others to their original owners. These riddles and dream guessings are lively and entertaining, providing a burst of frivolity in the midst of the serious activities.

This painting by Short Bull, an Oglala Lakota war chief, shows a Lakota Sun Dance. A warrior in the center of the painting is engaging in a ritual self-torture wherein he places skewers through the skin of his chest, ties them to a pole with long thongs, then pulls against the thongs until the skewers rip free.

The last section of Midwinter consists of the Four Sacred Rituals, given to the Iroquois by the creator. These rituals include dances and chants and end with a dance intended to thank Our Life Supporters—the spirits of the corn, beans, and squash upon which the Iroquois traditionally depended for their survival.

The Kwakiutls of British Columbia also perform important religious ceremonies during the winter. The most complex and spectacular winter ceremonial is known as Hamatsa (ha-MAT-sa). It is conducted by members of a secret dance society that is also called Hamatsa. The Hamatsas are men who are believed to be the survivors of encounters with a powerful deity that eats humans and is named Cannibal Spirit. The Hamatsa ritual centers on a man who wishes to be initiated into the secret society. The initiate is abducted by Cannibal Spirit and held in his dwelling in the forest. During this time, the initiate takes on Cannibal Spirit's powers and his appetite for human flesh. The initiate remains in the woods for several days, fasting, bathing in cold water, and rubbing his body with pine branches in order to make himself both physically and spiritually strong.

In a state of wild excitement, the possessed initiate returns to his village, clad only in wreaths of pine or hemlock branches, his face darkened with charcoal and blood. Over the next several days, he makes brief appearances in the village before running quickly back to his dwelling in the woods. Each night during this period, members of the Hamatsa society perform rituals aimed at bringing the initiate back into society and healing his troubled soul. Eventually, during one of his forays into the village, the initiate enters the Hamatsa ceremonial house through an opening in the roof. As he descends, the Hamatsas try to catch him and calm him, but still possessed by Cannibal Spirit, he wrestles free of their grasp and escapes into the darkness of the forest. Similar struggles are repeated on three additional nights, all symbolizing the eternal struggle between the forces of life, society, and order represented by the Hamatsa society, and the forces of death, wildness, and chaos represented by Cannibal Spirit, in whose fearsome clutches the initiate remains.

Finally, the initiate returns to the rooftop and enters the house through a large screen painted with an image of the Cannibal Spirit's mouth. The Hamatsas take hold of the initiate and do not release him. The leader of the Hamatsa society performs a purifying ritual that calms the initiate while others in attendance blow whistles and sing songs. At last, the man is properly reconciled with his family and community.

The Hamatsa ritual is a community event filled with power and drama. Its emotional effects on participants and audience alike are described by the words of James Sewid, a Kwakiutl whose autobiography recounts his initiation into the Hamatsa society. Sewid wrote:

> I lowered myself halfway into the house and showed half of my body to the crowd. I was making the hamatsa noise and I could see all the people standing up and swaying their hands, which is the way they would greet one another. Some of them were chanting and beating with sticks and there was a terrific noise that I heard up there. I had a strange feeling when they received me that night as I was hanging down through the roof. They were all chanting the songs and swaying their hands. I don't know how to express it, but it was a wonderful feeling to see all the people swaying their hands at me. . . .
>
> The people were all down there chanting and about thirty or forty people were beating the drums and sticks. It was out of this world what they were doing, and I can't express how I felt. It made me feel funny, made me feel out of this world. . . . And all the hamatsas from the different villages were there with a big strong blanket to receive me. I jumped onto this blanket . . . and I'll never forget that when I came through my mother was crying. She just cried and cried because I guess she thought it was so real that I had come back to civilization again after I had been away so long.

Among the Lakotas, Cheyennes, Blackfeet, Shoshones, Arapahos, and most other tribes of the Great Plains, the annual renewal ceremony occurs during the summertime. This ceremony, called the Sun Dance, traditionally took place when large groups of people camped together in early summer prior to communal buffalo hunts. Although the buffalo hunts are no longer held, the Sun

Dance is still conducted in its proper season. The performance of the Sun Dance varies among different peoples, but certain themes and activities are common throughout the region. In most cases, an individual sponsor makes a pledge to organize the Sun Dance on behalf of the community. Sponsors may make their pledges as a result of some personal or familial misfortune. For example, if a person or one of his or her relatives is seriously ill, the person might vow to sponsor the dance if the illness is cured. In this case, the ceremony is performed both as a reward and a thanksgiving to the deities for the cure. Sun Dances are also pledged in response to spirit messages revealed in dreams or other omens from the spirit world. Although each year's Sun Dance is sponsored by an individual, its purpose is to restore health and well-being to the entire community, as well as to restore the productive forces of nature themselves.

Plans for a Sun Dance begin months before the actual performance. The sponsor selects a ritualist to oversee the dance, and men in the community volunteer to dance in the ceremony. From that time until the dance begins, the men must periodically pray and purify their bodies and minds with sweat baths and fasting. The Sun Dance itself spans four days, preceded by several days of preparation. The first preparatory task is selecting a tree to serve as the center pole in the circular Sun Dance Lodge. The tree is ritually chosen, cut down, and brought to the community. After it is erected in the center of an open space, the rest of the lodge is built around it. The circular shape of the lodge has its own religious significance, representing the circular shape of the earth and, more abstractly, symbolizing the cyclical path of life and the cyclical changes in the seasons.

During the four days of the actual ceremonial, men and women participate by dancing, singing, and drumming within the sacred space of the Sun Dance Lodge. Prayers are offered to the spirit world, asking for community health, prosperity, and supernatural protection and offering thanks for the abundance of the past year. The dance sponsor may give expensive gifts to the participants. Originally, warriors would seek visions by cutting their own flesh or injuring themselves in some other fashion, but this is rarely practiced today.

The Midwinter, Hamatsa, and Sun Dance are all public ceremonies aimed at renewing the earth and society as a whole. The individuals who participate in these rituals, however, are also affected emotionally, physically, and economically—sometimes profoundly so. Likewise, rituals commemorating the events and achievements of individuals are seen as promoting the well-being of the entire community—and sometimes of the entire world as well. ▲

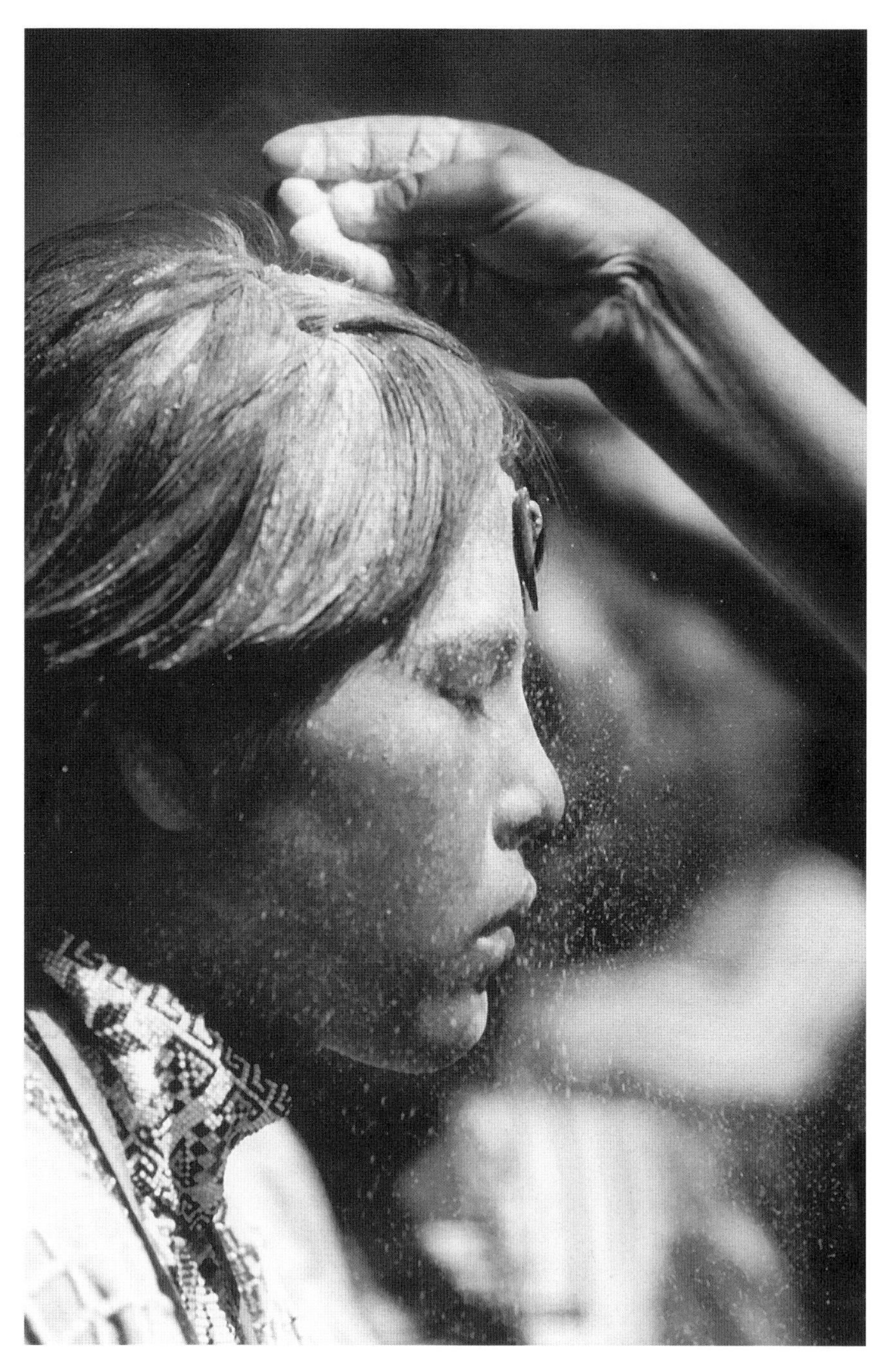

An Apache girl is sprinkled with pollen during her puberty ceremony. Important stages in people's personal and social development are often marked with special religious ceremonies in Native American cultures.

THE CYCLES OF LIFE

Like all peoples, Native Americans perform sometimes elaborate ceremonies to mark the significant phases of a person's life. Birth, naming, puberty, marriage, and death are all honored by rituals that celebrate the individual, the family, and the community. Although each Native American culture interprets the various stages of life in its own way, certain themes are commonly expressed. For example, rituals of birth and naming are usually aimed at obtaining spiritual protection for the child. Puberty ceremonies for girls generally celebrate their physiological readiness for motherhood. Boys' puberty is seldom marked by specific rituals, but in some societies teenage boys are expected to demonstrate their readiness for adulthood by seeking spirit guardians. Native American weddings usually emphasize the joining of individuals and families in a special bond and also serve as a form of public recognition of the new household. Finally, funerals express the sorrow of surviving relatives and friends and mark the departure of the deceased's soul to the afterworld.

Special activities marking the birth of a baby often start months before the actual delivery. Many Native Americans believe that parents-to-be should observe certain taboos on their behavior in order to protect their baby. For example, Inuit mothers and fathers carefully prevent their laces and belts from becoming knotted because if a knot occurs the baby may be strangled by the umbilical cord as it is born. Pregnant women of the Fox tribe were forbidden to touch a dead person, and if they looked at a corpse, they had to do so straight on because it was believed that if a pregnant woman glanced at a corpse with a slanted gaze, the baby would be born cross-eyed. Whenever a pregnant Fox woman carried a load of firewood, she was supposed to carry it on her back

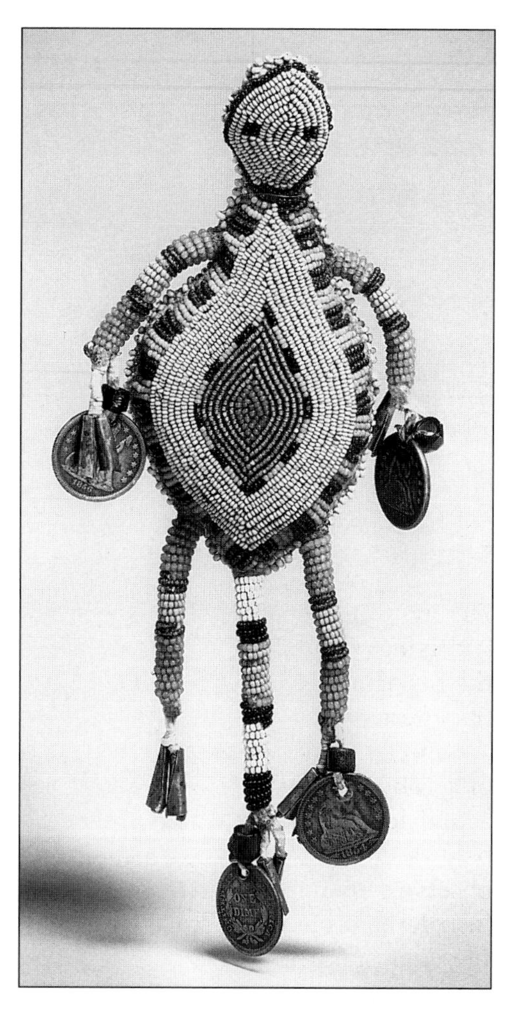

A turtle-shaped Lakota pouch, made of leather, beads, and coins, holds a baby's umbilical cord. People kept pouches containing their cords as a charm against misfortune.

rather than in her arms in order to assure an easy delivery. Among the Shoshones, a father-to-be does not eat meat during his wife's pregnancy; instead, he eats lightly and drinks a great deal of water in order to help his wife have an easy delivery. The link between father and child is further emphasized when the baby receives its first bath, at which time the father must take a dip in a creek (a bath that is usually a good deal colder than the child's).

In most Native American societies, a normal birth is not surrounded by ritual. If the birth is especially difficult and poses danger to mother and child, however, spiritual aid may be sought through rites, prayers, and offerings. One such birth was described in an autobiography of a Fox woman, recorded in 1918 when she was quite elderly. The birth of her first child was difficult, and a number of rituals were performed to aid her:

> When that woman [the healer] came, she at once boiled some medicine. After she had boiled it, she said: "Let her in any case sit up for a while. You must hold her so that she will not fall over." After I was made to sit up, she spat upon my head; and she gave me [medicine] to drink. After she had given me [medicine] to drink, she began singing. She started to go out singing and went around the little wickiup [hut] singing. When she danced by where I was, she knocked on the side. "Come out if you are a boy," she would say. And she would again begin singing. When she danced by she again knocked the side. "Come out if you are a girl," she would say again. After she sang four times in a circle, she entered [the wickiup]. And she gave me [medicine] to drink. "Now it will be born. She may lie down. . . ." Lo, sure enough, a little boy was born.

Many Native Americans believe that spiritual connections exist between newborn babies and their ancestors. The Haidas of British Columbia believe that babies are reincarnations of deceased relatives. The specific relative reincarnated can be identified by a particular physical resemblance or personality trait exhibited by the baby, or sometimes people near death can foretell their own reincarnations. Florence Edenshaw Davidson, a Haida woman, recalled in her autobiography that she was her father's favorite child because she was the reincarnation of her father's mother:

> My dad used to favor me because I used to tell him, *"Hada, ding awu di ijing,"* "Dad, I'm your mother." They used to believe in second-birth [reincarnation]. *"Hada, ding awu di ijing,"* I kept on saying. Those were my first words.

Davidson also reported that her deceased husband, Robert, was reincarnated. She said:

> Right before my husband died, he said to our granddaughter who was pregnant. "Joy, I'm coming back to you. I'm going to be real handsome and real smart, too." Craig, her son, is the second birth of my husband.

In most Native American societies, babies do not receive their names immediately after birth. Parents wait a specified period of time, perhaps as short as four days or as long as several months. The choice of a name is usually dictated by a tribe's traditions. A common practice among peoples of the Great Plains is for parents to ask a respected elder to choose a name for their child. Elders select names prompted by a sight or sound that appears spontaneously when they are pondering the choice, or the name may come to the elder in a dream or vision. Plains names often refer to animals, birds, or material objects, such as the names of the well-known 19th-century Lakota leaders Sitting Bull and Crazy Horse or the 19th-century Crow medicine woman Pretty Shield.

In many Native American cultures (including those of the Plains Indians), people of all ages may receive additional names that reflect their physical appearances, personality traits, accomplishments, or religious experiences. Names by which individuals are known may change several times during their lives. New names are sometimes given in hopes of obtaining spiritual powers or protection. For instance, a 19th-century Hidatsa woman named Waheenee recounted in her autobiography the reasons for her name change from Good Way to Buffalo-Bird Woman:

> I was a rather sickly child and my father wished after a time to give me a new name. We Indians thought that sickness was from the gods. A child's name was given as a kind of prayer. A new name often moved the gods to help a sick or weakly child.
>
> So my father gave me another name, Waheenee-wea, or Buffalo-Bird Woman. My father's gods were birds; and these, we thought, had much holy power. Perhaps the

> buffalo-birds had spoken to him in a dream.
>
> I am still called by the name my father gave me; and, as I have lived to be a very old woman, I think it has brought me good luck from the gods.

The naming of a child is often surrounded by actions and prayers intended to bring the child health and long life. For example, Tewa babies are named on the fourth day after birth in a ceremony performed by the infant's naming mother, one of the two midwives who assisted the mother during delivery. At dawn, the naming mother takes the child outside and lifts it toward the rising sun while her assistant makes circular motions with a small handbroom to sweep in blessings for the child. The naming mother announces the child's name and offers a prayer to the spirits:

> Here is a child who has been given to us
> Let us bring him/her to manhood and womanhood
> You who are dawn youths and dawn maidens
> You who are winter spirits
> You who are summer spirits
> We have brought out a child that you may bring to manhood and womanhood
> That you may give long life
> Give him/her good fortune we ask of you.

The Iroquois bestow names on children during either of two annual communal rituals, the Midwinter ceremonial in January or the Green Corn ceremony in July. By giving names in the context of communal rituals, the Iroquois highlight the fact that children are recognized not only as members of families but also as members of a large and supportive community.

Among societies of the Pacific Coast in Canada, names have great personal, social, and religious significance. Peoples such as the Kwakiutls, Haidas, and Tsimshians (CHIM-shins) of British Columbia give children names that reflect a complex system of inherited social status or rank. The ranks are associated with supernatural powers and protections as well as with wealth, social prestige, and political leadership. Most babies receive only one name, but people of high social standing bestow many names on their children, particularly on eldest sons. Each name belongs to a specific family and therefore represents a long social history. Names are given to babies during rituals called *potlatches*, which are ceremonial feasts sponsored by a family for a variety of occasions including naming, puberty, marriage, and death. When parents of high rank name their baby, they hold an elaborate potlatch and invite their peers to witness the child's introduction to society. In his autobiography, James Sewid, the eldest son of wealthy and prestigious Kwakiutl parents, recalled that he was given an array of valuable names:

> I received my father's father's name from the Kwiksutainuk people,

A Kwakiutl potlatch held at Alert Bay, British Columbia, around 1900. The basins, kettles, cloths, and other goods pictured here were distributed to guests.

> Owadziki, which means "people will do anything for him because he is so respected." My mother's father . . . was from the Mamalilikulla people and I received the name Poogleedee from him, which means "guests never leave his feasts hungry." I received the name Waltkeena which was from Chief Goatlas of the Mamalilikulla and means "something very precious has been given to us." I received the name Sewid after my father and his father, which means, "paddling towards the chief that is giving a potlatch."

These names were all given shortly after James was born. Ten months later, a second potlatch was held in his honor at which time he received additional names from paternal and maternal relatives. His names have meanings such as "you are proud of what you have done in potlatching," "he always wants to share his wealth with others," "always giving away wealth," "when the guests arrive for a potlatch they are all welcomed at his house," and "he is wealthy from many generations back."

In addition to naming rituals, other ceremonies may take place during childhood. Among the southwestern tribes, children are initiated into ceremonial groups known as kachina societies, named after powerful deities called *kachinas* (ka-CHEE-nas). The Zunis only initiate boys into the societies (although grown women can join), while among the Hopis and the Tewas, both girls and boys are initiated into kachina groups. Initiation is highly valued because before that time children are not allowed to participate in or witness most rituals.

Hopi initiations, called *kachinvaki*, are conducted each year for groups of girls and boys who are between six and nine years old. Parents choose ceremonial mothers or fathers who will sponsor the initiation for their children. This sponsor encourages the child to behave properly, treat other people with kindness, and respect and honor the spirits. At the appointed time, the sponsor leads the child to the *kiva* (KEY-va), a ceremonial building where the initiation is held.

The ritual is conducted by adult male members of the kachina society. In preparation, they dress in masks and costumes to impersonate kachina deities and wait outside the village. When all the children have arrived at the kiva, the masked kachinas enter the kiva making sudden gestures and loud noises to frighten the young children, who have

A group of Zuni kachina impersonators perform a dance in a village plaza in 1899. Although impersonators are not considered deities, they are believed to take on some of the powers of the kachinas that they imitate.

never before been in the presence of powerful spirits. One of the kachinas carries branches of yucca, a plant that grows wild in the desert. Another kachina takes four yucca branches and whips each of the children four times. Most of the children receive light or moderate blows and are not hurt, but boys who are known to be unruly may be strongly whipped. After the floggings end, the kachinas whip each other, an act which undoubtedly gives the children some satisfaction.

The kachinas return the next day and perform dances for the children and their sponsors. At the end of the dances, the kachina figures take off their masks so that the children can see that the kachinas are actually their relatives and neighbors. The children are often shocked and disappointed to learn that the beings they had always thought were gods are in fact humans. Dan Talayesva, a Hopi chief, recalled his youthful experience:

> That night everybody went to the kiva to see the kachinas dance. When the kachinas entered the kiva without masks, I had a great surprise. They were not spirits, but human beings. I recognized nearly every one of them and felt very unhappy, because I had been told all my life that the kachinas were gods.

A Hopi woman, Helen Sekaquaptewa, had a similar reaction:

> It was quite an ordeal for me. When I went back to my home I wished I didn't know that a kachina was a man with a costume and a mask, when all the time I had thought they were real magic.

But the Hopi ritual leaders quickly explain to the children that even though living men impersonate kachinas, the kachina spirits themselves watch and approve the proceedings, and their powerful essence comes to the Hopis even though they are physically absent. In this way, the children learn that spiritual power exists and affects humans even though it cannot be seen, and they also learn that human participation is essential to maintaining good relations with the spirit world.

Many Native American societies celebrate girls' puberty by rituals that focus on fertility, preparation for adult responsibilities, and long life. The Western Apaches of Arizona call their puberty rite *nai'es,* which means "preparing her" or "getting her ready," reflecting the rite's central theme of readying the pubescent girl for adulthood and motherhood. The ceremony is given by the girl's family and attended by everyone in the community. Preparations begin immediately upon the girl's first menstruation, but the rite itself is not performed until summertime. The girl's parents select a ritualist to supervise the ceremony and choose a woman as a sponsor for their daughter.

The ceremony begins shortly after sunrise, a time of day that is considered spiritually powerful. It consists of several separate rituals, each of which is supposed to bring spiritual and material benefits to the girl. First, the girl dances in an open space. During this rite, the girl is transformed into the Apache deity of fertility and kindness, Changing Woman (also known as White Painted Woman), taking on her qualities and powers. The girl's assumption of Changing Woman's attributes is signified in the next part of the puberty rite, when she kneels on a buckskin blanket, raises her hands to her shoulders, and rocks back and forth in a symbolic imitation of the posture Changing Woman took when she had her first menstrual period and became ready for motherhood. Then the girl's ceremonial sponsor massages her body in order to mold her into a strong and energetic woman.

The final part of the ritual is focused on bringing blessings to the girl and her community. First, the supervising ritualist pours a basket of corn kernels and sweets over the girl's head and body,

An Apache girl and her attendants are sprinkled with corn pollen during her puberty ceremony.

symbolizing the good crops and wealth wished for the girl. Then the young girl and her sponsor dance in place on the buckskin blanket and are blessed by everyone present at the ceremony. These blessings do not only benefit the girl; since she has received powers from Changing Woman, she bestows health, good crops, and success on those who talk to her.

The puberty ritual ends when the young girl shakes out the buckskin blanket on which she has been dancing and throws it toward the four cardinal directions of east, south, west, and north. The rotation of movement through all directions symbolizes the cycle of human life from birth through a healthy long life. After the puberty ceremony is completed, the spiritual powers of Changing Woman remain in the girl's body for four additional days, and during this time, she can cure illness or bring rain.

While the biological maturity of boys is not usually specifically marked by rituals in Native American cultures, in many societies of the plains, prairies, and northern woodlands teenage boys participate in rituals called vision quests. During a vision quest, a boy seeks visions of a supernatural being who will become his personal guardian. (In some societies, girls also seek visions.) After a boy decides to go on a vision quest, he usually spends four days fasting and praying for supernatural guidance. As a final act of preparation, he purifies himself by undergoing a sweat bath in a small windowless hut containing heated stones. Sweat baths are considered sacred and are supposed to cleanse people of physical and psychological impurities to better prepare them for the world of supernatural beings. Once the sweat bath is finished, the quester is ready to concentrate on spiritual matters.

The boy begins his vision quest by leaving his community and retreating to an isolated place where he typically remains for four days. During this time, he stays awake, fasts, and drinks as little water as possible. He also prays to the spirit world, asking for supernatural protection and aid. Visions, when they come, can take many different forms. The quester may see an animal or an unusual natural phenomenon, or he may hear words or a song. A spirit may teach the quester special songs or rituals to perform when in danger or need. Or a quester may find a distinctive object such as an eagle feather, an oddly shaped stone, or an animal bone. Whatever is found during a vision quest is believed to have supernatural powers, and the quester can use this power to his advantage.

The vision quest (or any other visionary episode) is a profoundly meaningful religious experience. A 19th-century Lakota spiritual leader, Black Elk, once described his own quest in the woods, during which he was clad only with a buffalo robe for the cold nights and was briefly accompanied by a spiritual leader named Few Tails. Black Elk recalled:

> There was nobody there but the old man and myself and the sky and the

> earth. But the place was full of people; for the spirits were there. . . .
>
> It was time for me to begin lamenting, so Few Tails went away somewhere and left me there all alone on the hill with the spirits and the dying light.
>
> Standing in the center of the sacred place and facing the sunset, I began to cry, and while crying I had to say: "O Great Spirit, accept my offerings! O make me understand!"

Soon afterward, several omens appeared in the forms of a spotted eagle, a chicken hawk, and a black swallow. Then the first vision came:

> While I was crying, something was coming from the south. It looked like dust far off, but when it came closer, I saw it was a cloud of beautiful butterflies of all colors. They swarmed around me so thick that I could see nothing else.
>
> I walked backwards . . . and the spotted eagle on the pine tree spoke and said: "Behold these! They are your people. They are in great difficulty and you shall help them." Then I could hear all the butterflies that were swarming over me, and they were all making a pitiful, whimpering noise as though they too were weeping.

The successful completion of a vision quest not only provides the quester with powerful spiritual protection but also indicates and, in a sense, celebrates his ability to endure isolation and deprivation. This sort of endurance was an important survival skill for Native American men and women, who sometimes had to live through great physical and psychic hardships. Indeed, in many Native American cultures, children began toughening themselves at an early age, observing short fasts or exposing themselves to cold long before they were old enough to go on a vision quest. The vision quest thus demonstrates an individual's complete readiness for the perils and privations of adulthood.

Once Native Americans reach physical and social maturity, they are eligible to marry. In most Native American cultures, marriage is marked with formal exchanges of gifts between members of the bride's and groom's families. These exchanges are ritualized means of emphasizing the interconnection between the families as well as between the individuals. The presents are often symbolic of women's and men's roles in society. Iroquois women gave their mothers-in-law corn cakes, reflecting women's traditional role as farmers, while men gave their mothers-in-law deer meat, reflecting men's role as hunters. Following these gift exchanges, the bride's family would sponsor a public feast to honor the new couple.

The details of wedding ceremonies vary greatly from tribe to tribe. Navajo weddings consist of prayers for the health, fertility, long life, and beauty of the bride and groom. Toward the end of the marriage ceremony, the couple eats a mixture of white and yellow corn sprinkled with corn pollen. The color white represents maleness while the

Black Elk, a 19th-century Lakota religious leader whose life and spiritual experiences, including his vision quest, were recorded in the autobiographical Black Elk Speaks.

color yellow represents femaleness, and the mixture of the two corns symbolizes the joining of husband and wife. Weddings in Pacific Northwest societies are usually occasions for potlatches and displays of family wealth. The families of the wedded couple give away large quantities of gifts to the guests, including dishes, carved boxes, and clothing.

Funerals give rise to the most intense and solemn rituals in many Native American societies. These rituals serve several religious and social purposes. They allow members of the deceased's family to express their grief in a socially acceptable fashion, and the concern shown by others in the community reminds the family members that, while they may have lost a loved one, they are still part of a caring, supportive network. Funerals also serve a spiritual purpose in preparing the dead for their journey to the afterworld. Food, clothing, ornaments, small tools, and utensils are often buried with the dead for their use in the afterlife.

Many Native American religions teach that the souls of the dead remain near their earthly homes for a period of time, usually four days. The soul is then ready to depart on its spirit journey. In some cases, special rites are held both to protect the living from harmful contact with the dead and to release the deceased's soul so that it can make its final departure. Among the Tewas, the last act in a long series of funeral rites is called the releasing. Offerings of food and tobacco smoke are made to the soul at spirit shrines, and then a ritualist who conducts the ceremony draws four lines on the ground, spits out bits of charcoal that he has held in his mouth, and utters a final prayer to the deceased in which he urges the soul to bestow blessings and good fortune on the people:

> We have muddied the waters for you [the tobacco smoke]
> We have cast shadows between us [the charcoal]
> We have made steep gullies between us [the lines]
> Do not, therefore, reach for even a hair on our heads
> Rather, help us attain that which we are always seeking
> Long life, that our children may grow
> Abundant game, the raising of crops
> And in all the works of man
> Ask for these things for all, and do no more
> And now you must go, for you are now free.

The Hurons conducted both individual and communal rituals for the dead. When an individual died, a funeral was held three days later to honor his or her soul. Relatives of the deceased mourned deeply, with loud crying and lamenting. Community members came to the funeral, bringing gifts to be buried with the deceased or to be distributed to the deceased's relatives "to dry their tears." Following the funeral, the deceased's spouse entered a period of intense mourning that lasted 10 days. During that time, the spouse lay only on thin mats with his or her face against the ground, did not speak to anyone, ate only cold food, rarely went outdoors, and had disheveled hair and an unkempt appearance. After this period of mourning ended, spouses continued mourning in a less intense fashion for a year, speaking quietly and refraining from participation in public festivities.

In addition to these individual mourning practices, the Hurons performed a solemn community ritual called the Feast of the Dead. The feast was held once every 10 years to commemorate all Huron deaths that occurred since the previous rite. During the Feast of the Dead, the women of the tribe exhumed the bones of their deceased relatives from their individual graves, wrapped the bones in beaver skins, and carried them in a mournful procession to a site in one of the villages where a communal grave had been dug. When all the Hurons had assembled there, the bones were ceremoniously placed in the grave and covered over with presents, beaver skins, and earth—bringing together the entire nation, honoring all of their ancestors, and dramatically underscoring the sense of community and unity essential to Huron society.

Native American rituals honor the unique character of each stage of life, as well as the interwoven texture of the entire cycle of human existence. But between birth and death there is often sickness and pain, and disease can easily shorten a life. While the above-mentioned rituals mark the normal stages of life, the exceptional circumstances of illnesses require a different kind of ceremony—ceremonies designed especially to combat disease.▲

A Tlinkit healer performs a rite over an ill man. Most traditional Native American societies assign supernatural causes to diseases.

HEALTH AND HEALING

In the 1920s, an Inuit man named Aua took the Danish researcher Knud Rasmussen to the home of his sister Natseq, who was gravely ill. Aua spoke solemnly to Rasmussen of his sister's illness:

> Why must people be ill and suffer pain? We are all afraid of illness. Here is this old sister of mine; as far as anyone can see, she has done no evil; she has lived through a long life and given birth to healthy children, and now she must suffer before her days end. Why? Why?

Aua's question has been repeated across all cultures throughout human history. All humans face the possibility of illness, which sometimes brings intense pain and premature death, and many people wonder why they and their loved ones should suffer.

Various cultures have come up with equally varied explanations for illnesses in an attempt to understand, avoid, and cure disease. In many cultures, including traditional Native American cultures, certain ailments are thought to have spiritual or supernatural causes. Common ailments, such as minor sore throats, earaches, indigestion, and muscle aches and pains, are rarely considered to have spiritual causes and are often treated by laypeople with traditional remedies such as herbs or massage. But illnesses that involve severe pain or unusual symptoms or that do not respond to ordinary remedies may be believed to be caused by supernatural forces. Such illnesses need to be treated by healers who have special spiritual powers and knowledge of the supernatural realm and who are trained in many diagnostic and medical skills. These healers observe patients' symptoms, discuss relevant aspects of patients' activities, and employ ritual means to learn the impact of the spiritual realm on their patients' health.

Native American healers acquire their curing powers in many different ways. Some actively seek spiritual knowledge by praying or questing for visions, some learn their skills by becoming apprentices to practicing doctors, and others get power spontaneously either in dreams or in visions. Isaac Tens, a Gitskan healer in British Columbia, recounted his experiences with supernatural power that led him to learn doctoring skills:

> Thirty years after my birth . . . I went up into the hills to get fire-wood. While I was cutting up the wood into lengths, it drew dark towards the evening. Before I had finished my last stack of wood, a loud noise broke out over me, . . . and a large owl appeared to me. The owl took hold of me, caught my face, and tried to lift me up. I lost consciousness. As soon as I came back to my senses I realized that I had fallen into the snow. My head was coated with ice, and some blood was running out of my mouth.
>
> I stood up and went down the trail, walking very fast. . . . On my way, the trees seemed to shake and to lean over me; tall trees were crawling after me, as if they had been snakes. I could see them. Before I arrived at my father's home, I told my folk what had happened to me, as soon as I walked in. I was very cold and warmed myself before going to bed. There I fell into a sort of trance. It seems that two *halaaits* [healers] were working over me to bring me back to health. But it is now all vague in my memory. . . .
>
> While I was in a trance, one of [the *halaaits*] told me that the time had arrived for me to become a *halaait* like them. But I did not agree; so I took no notice of the advice. . . .
>
> Another time, I went to my hunting grounds on the other side of the river. . . . Farther along I looked for a bear's den amid the tall trees. As I glanced upwards, I saw an owl, at the top of a high cedar. I shot it, and it fell down in the bushes close to me. When I went to pick it up, it had disappeared. Not a feather was left; this seemed very strange. I walked down to the river, crossed over the ice, and returned to the village. . . . I met my father who had just come out to look for me, for he had missed me. We went back together to my house. Then my heart started to beat fast, and I began to tremble, just as had happened a while before, when the *halaaits* were trying to fix me up. My flesh seemed to be boiling. . . . My body was quivering. While I remained in this state, I began to sing. A chant was coming out of me without my being able to do anything to stop it. Many things appeared to me presently: huge birds and other animals. They were calling me. . . . Such visions occur when a man is about to become a *halaait*; they occur of their own accord. The songs force themselves out complete without any attempt to compose them.

Sanapia, a Comanche healer, was trained in her skills by her mother and mother's brother. Both relatives were a type of healer known as eagle doctors, who possess curing powers derived from eagle spirits. Among the Coman-

An Assiniboin man holds a slain eagle. Many Plains Indians believe that eagle spirits possess great healing power.

ches, healers usually select their successors from among close kin, generally passing medical knowledge from mother to daughter. Although Sanapia's training came from her relatives, her healing ability comes from supernatural helpers, especially the eagle spirits. Her helpers appear in dreams and visions and teach her songs and prayers to use when she cures. Sanapia readily credits the eagle spirits as her source of healing power:

> The eagle got more power than anything living, I guess. Its got Medicine to help people get well . . . to cure them. I got power like that eagle because the eagle help me when I call on it when I doctor. My mother told me that I be just like that eagle when I doctor. I can feel the eagle working in me when I doctor and try hard to get somebody well.

Beliefs about supernatural causes of illness vary among Native American societies. In some cultures, illness is thought to result from a patient's prior actions or from contact with harmful objects or forces, while in others, spirit beings are believed to inflict sickness on people as a punishment for wrongdoings. In some cultures, malevolent human witches or sorcerers are believed to be able to cause illness. But in all cultures, diagnosis of an ailment's cause is crucial to deciding on a course of treatment. Once a diagnosis is made, a healer can perform ceremonies to eliminate the underlying causative factors. Although most cures are effective, some treatments fail, leading to prolonged illness and eventual death. When this occurs, it is usually blamed on the healers' skills, which are considered too weak to counteract the supernatural forces that caused the disease.

The Inuits believe that illness sometimes results from actions that have offended supernatural beings. If men fail to properly honor the spirits of the animals they hunt or if women fail to abide by taboos during pregnancy, they may become ill. People also may get sick if they have been uncooperative, argumentative, or bad-tempered. When patients do not respond to simple treatments, the Inuit healer asks them to review their past behavior. If a patient recalls some wrongful act, he or she publicly admits the error, and the healer gives the patient rules to follow for a specified period of time. A patient may be told to abstain from eating certain foods or to throw away articles of clothing or household goods.

The Iroquois also believe that some illnesses result from people's thoughts and actions. However, their theory of disease stresses the role of an individual's inner wishes as a possible cause of ailments. They think that one's inner wishes are expressed in dreams and that in order to maintain good health, people must satisfy these wishes. If people deny their own desires, they may become ill. Therefore, Iroquois healers often ask patients to recall their dreams. In some cases, the wishes expressed in dreams are overt and obvious. For example, a patient may remember dreaming about

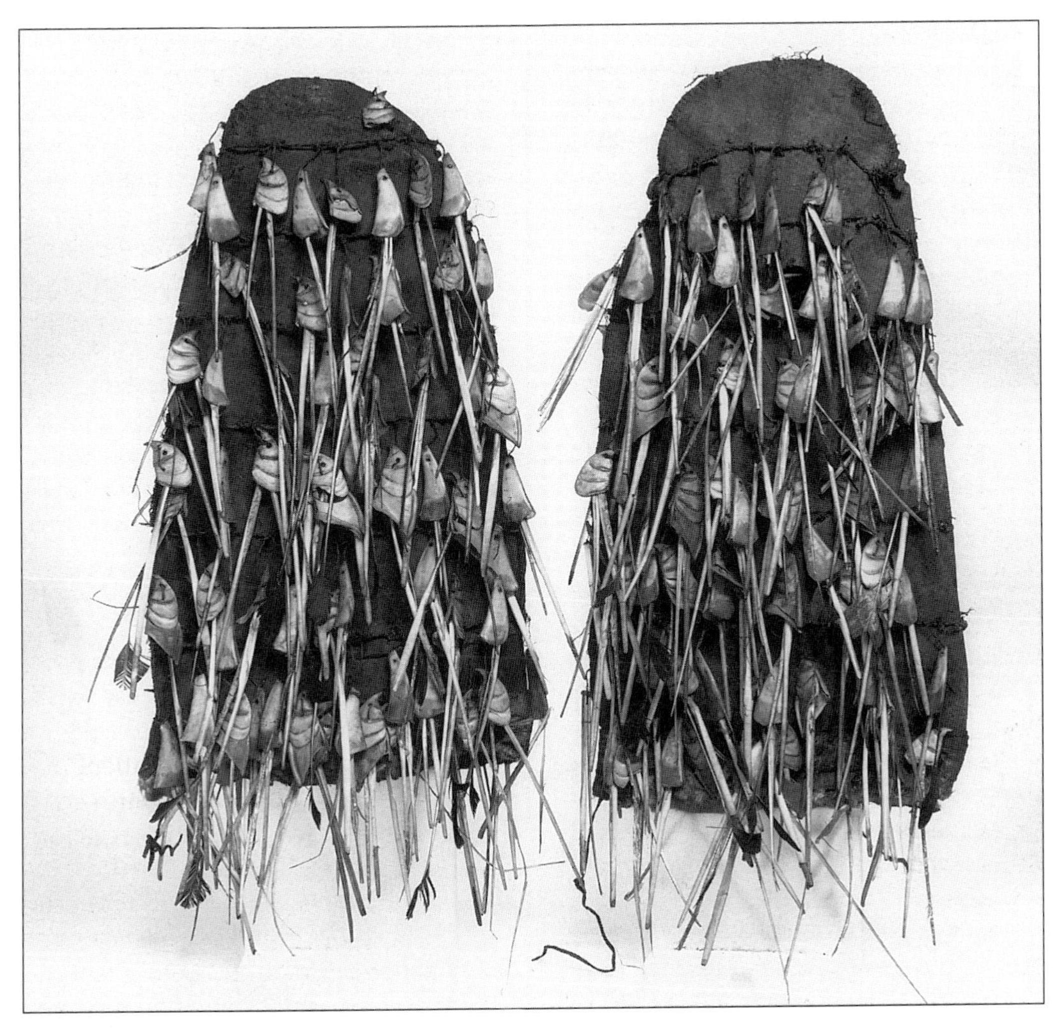

A pair of Inuit sealskin gloves, decorated with horned puffin beaks and bird quills.

receiving a particular present, visiting with a relative or friend, or attending a specific kind of ceremony. When this occurs, members of the community attempt to satisfy the patient's wishes by giving the desired gift, arranging for the relative or friend to visit, or performing the desired ceremony.

In other cases, however, the patient's wish is not so obvious. When this occurs, the patient seeks the aid of a healer who specializes in determining hidden desires. These healers use a number of ritual techniques to receive messages from the spirit realm concerning the patient's wish, including gazing in water or fire, fasting, or entering a trance state in an attempt to see images of the desire. Once the wish has been determined, the patient and his or her family attempt to fulfill it.

Several Native American theories of disease are based on the belief that an illness can result from the loss of an individual's soul. According to the Inuits, the soul normally leaves the body during sleep and returns just before the sleeper awakens. If a soul does not come back because it is lost or has been captured or harmed by evil spirits or witches, the individual will become gravely ill and will eventually die. Symptoms of soul loss include a depletion of energy and appetite, insomnia, or depression. These cases must be dealt with swiftly in order to save the patient's life.

A patient suffering from soul loss is treated by a spiritual healer called an *angakot,* who attempts to retrieve the lost soul by using a dramatic and emotionally intense ritual. This ritual takes place at night in a darkened house, where all the lights are extinguished and the windows and doorways are covered. The patient lies on a mat while family and community members gather before him or her. The angakot takes a place behind the patient and proceeds to summon spiritual helpers—cooperative souls of ghosts, animals, and supernatural beings that the angakot has acquired over the years through prayers, dreams, and other spiritual means. After singing and drumming for a period of time, the angakot enters a trance state and speaks to his or her helpers in a special language, commanding them to join the healer on a spirit journey to seek the patient's lost soul. Along the way, they encounter evil creatures trying to block their path and they must fight them in order to locate and rescue the lost soul. Patients and their families can often hear the loud shouts and moans of the angakot, the helpers, and the malicious creatures during these battles. At the end of a successful ritual cure, the angakot retrieves the patient's soul and returns it to the patient's body. Patients usually experience feelings of tremendous emotional relief when their souls are returned to them, and recovery from the illness quickly follows.

Many Native American peoples believe that disease can be caused by the intrusion of foreign objects, particles, or substances into human bodies, which must be located and extracted in order to restore health. These foreign objects are believed to disrupt the inner physical and psychic harmony and balance necessary to good health. Supernatural beings may shoot these objects into a victim's body as a punishment for a failure to show respect to the spirits or a neglect of ritual rules. Human witches also shoot objects into someone to retaliate for a real or imagined slight.

Shoshone and Comanche healers of the western plains have several techniques for extracting foreign objects hidden in a patient's body. Disease-causing objects include tiny feathers, pebbles, bits of animal bone, or a special amorphous liquid substance without particu-

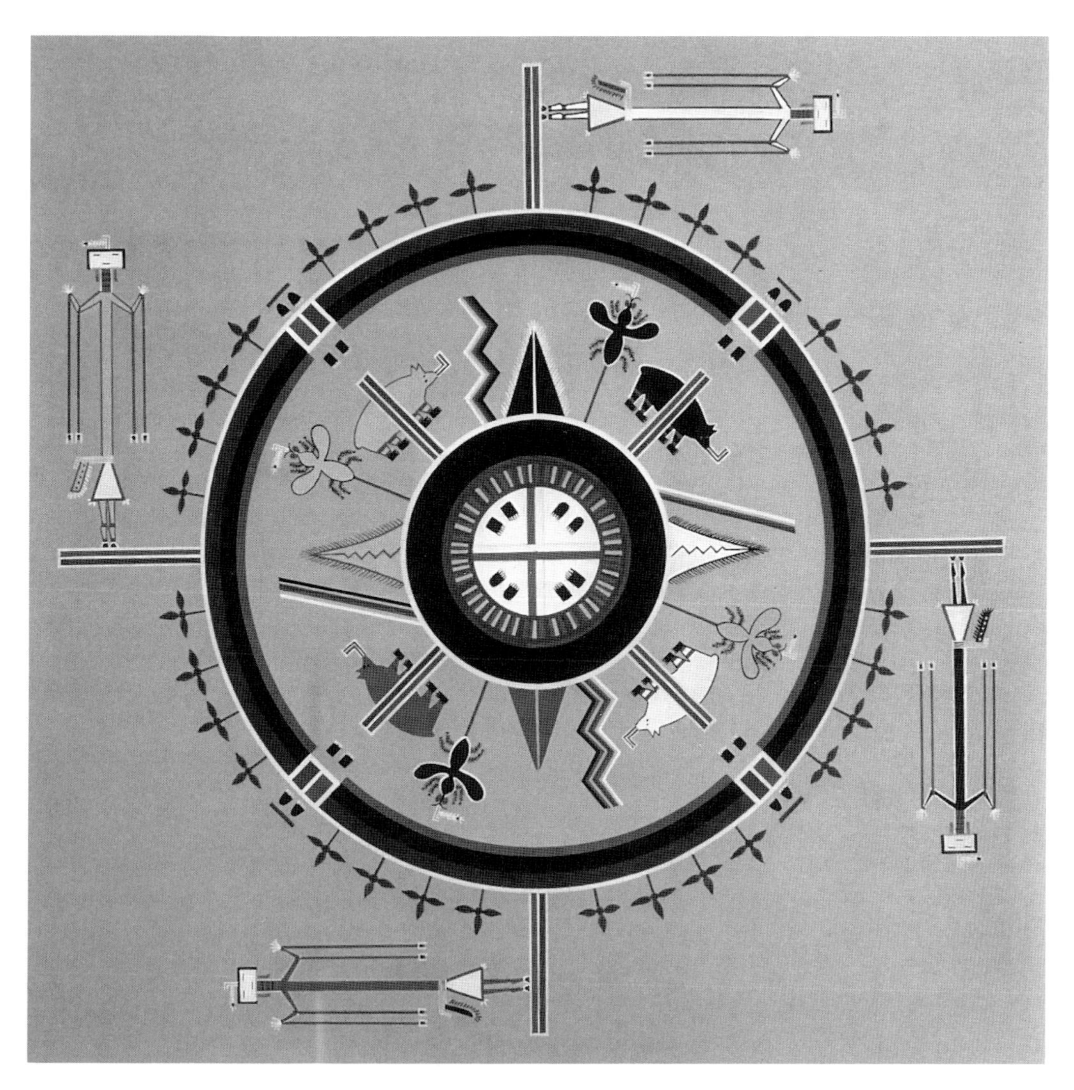

This Navajo sandpainting, used in a healing ceremony, includes four bears emanating from the circle at the center of the painting. While the Navajos believe that accidental contact with bears can cause illness, the special powers of the bear can be used to encourage healing.

lar shape, and they produce a variety of symptoms, such as localized pain, swelling, or stiffness. Healers often begin by gently massaging the afflicted area, then they remove the object by sucking on the spot. Once retrieved, the object is spat out and thrown into a fire or otherwise ritually purified and discarded.

The Navajos believe that people can become sick if they have had contact with a contaminating object, being, or force. Numerous animals, insects, and plants can potentially cause illness, including bears, porcupines, coyotes, rattlesnakes, ants, moths, and cacti. Natural forces such as lightning and whirlwinds are also dangerous. The Navajo theory of contamination is based on their belief that health requires the maintenance of internal and external balances. Certain objects, animals, or natural forces cause disruptions in a person's normal balance, which leads to disease if not properly counteracted. Consequently, treatment aims at removing the harmful effects of contamination and restoring the body to its normal state of harmony and beauty.

Navajo healers are skilled in the long and elaborate rituals that cure patients of contaminating entities. The rituals, called chantways or sings, are of many types, depending upon the specific cause of the patient's illness. In general, sings produce cures by attracting the spiritual powers of the Holy People, the deities of the Navajos. Curing sings last two, five, or nine nights, a night being counted from sunset until the following sunset. Each sing consists of separate rites that must be performed in a specific order. Sings often begin with a cleansing bath for the patient, followed by prayers and chants to attract Holy People and to motivate them to use their great powers to remove the harmful effects of the contaminating agents.

Navajo healers also possess ritual paraphernalia that have healing powers, including feather wands, painted prayer sticks, small pieces of turquoise and crystal, cornmeal, corn pollen, and herbal medicines. Healers touch these powerful objects to a patient's body, transferring their curative forces to the patient. In addition, Navajo healers attract and transfer beneficial supernatural powers by the use of dry paintings, which are images made with sand colored with different pigments. Healers sprinkle the colored sand on the ground in complex designs to produce stylized images of Holy People. Most dry paintings are about 6 feet in diameter, although some are as large as 20 feet across. When the dry painting is completed, the patient sits on a portion of the painting. The healer moistens his or her palm with medicinal water and touches the painting so that the colored sand adheres to his or her hand. The healer then applies the sand to the patient's body and repeats this process using sand from different portions of the painting and applying it to comparable parts of the patient's body.

The dry painting rite acts out the Navajo's philosophical emphasis on the wholeness of the body. A patient's pain may appear to be localized, but since the disharmony of disease affects the entire body and mind, the patient's whole body is treated. Since the external environment also has an effect on human health, natural forces must be kept in balance as well. The following excerpt

This drawing from the 1880s shows a group of Zunis torturing a witch. Among the Zunis, practicing witchcraft (a crime that legally encompassed not only the casting of evil spells but also a variety of less magical criminal acts, including murder) could be punished by ostracism from the tribe or execution.

from a long healing prayer demonstrates the all-inclusiveness of the Navajo medical system:

> I have made your sacrifice.
> I have prepared a smoke for you.
> My feet restore for me.
> My legs restore for me.
> My body restore for me.
> My mind restore for me. . . .
> Impervious to pain, may I walk.
> Feeling light within, may I walk.
> With lively feelings, may I walk.
> Happily may I walk.
> Happily abundant dark clouds I desire.
> Happily abundant showers I desire.
> Happily abundant vegetation I desire.
> Happily abundant pollen I desire.
> Happily abundant dew I desire. . . .
> May it be happy before me.
> May it be happy behind me.
> May it be happy below me.
> May it be happy above me.
> With it happy all around me, may I walk.
> It is finished in beauty. . . .
> It is finished in beauty.

Another theory of disease (often found in conjunction with the theories mentioned above) maintains that illness and other misfortunes can be caused by witches or sorcerers. Witches and sorcerers are humans who perform harmful magic because they are malicious, aggressive, jealous, and spiteful. They magically attack people who have slighted them, and since they are jealous and oversensitive, they may do evil against innocent people who have done them no harm. Each culture has different beliefs about how witches practice their arts. In general, they are thought to have access to supernatural powers that they acquire through prayers, visions, and dreams. They can also learn witchcraft from other practitioners, paying fees for their apprenticeship. In all cases, witches work in secret, since any society that accepts their existence also has very strong prohibitions against the practice of witchcraft and will persecute anyone who is proved to be a witch.

In many societies, people believe that witches may also be healers because the supernatural powers that enable people to cure disease are essentially neutral and can be used for malicious purposes as well. The Skokomishs of western Washington believe that healers (called doctors) can be responsible for both health and illness. If doctors want to harm someone, they may shoot foreign objects into victims or extract their life-soul. One Skokomish gave an account of an evil doctor's practice:

> Doctors used their powers to kill people by shooting sticks into them, or they'd go to people when they were sleeping and draw their life-soul out of them, pull it out of their heads, and hide it in the graveyard. Or they'd wrap the life-soul in cedar bark and hang it in the smoke of the fire in their houses and make you awful sick and kill you. It was dangerous to shoot doctor power into a person, because another doctor might find it there and kill it, and that would kill the doctor that sent it.
>
> A big chief was dying, and they sent there and got Duke Williams

> to doctor him. And Duke found that man's life-soul all wrapped up in cedar bark and hanging in another man's house. And he brought it back with his spirit power, and washed it and put it back in the sick man, and that man got well.

The Apaches believe that witches have several techniques for causing illness and death. They may use poisons made from the skin of human corpses, bear feces, rattlesnake skin, and bits of wood taken from trees that have been struck by lightning. These poisons are put into victims' food, thrown into their houses, or dropped into their noses or mouths while they sleep. Witches can also cause illness by uttering malicious spells or thinking evil thoughts against their victim. Like spirits, they may shoot harmful objects into the victim's body. The following is an Apache narrative of a witchcraft incident:

> That time I was with X and we were working on the drift fence near that spotted mountain. At night, that time, X was by the fire eating his grub. He said to me: "I don't feel so good." Then he went to sleep. In the night he woke me up and said: "I was just sleeping there and I wake up with big pain right here, here in my neck. It sure hit me all of a sudden." Then that time later in the night, it hit him again. He said: "I wonder who is shooting at me?" Then I know that someone is after him with shooting sorcery.

When an ailment comes on suddenly, witchcraft is usually suspected. Witchcraft is also considered at fault if an illness does not respond to usual ritual treatments or if several people in a family get sick or die within a short period of time. Apaches who suffer from ailments caused by witchcraft are treated by rituals that remove the harmful spell and restore good health. If the cure successfully leads to the patient's recovery, the witch responsible will become ill from the same malady and die soon afterward.

Native American beliefs in supernatural causes and treatments of illness have a common theme. Faced with the unfortunate universal truth that all people get sick and die, people appeal to the spirit world to learn the reasons for life and death and ways of coping with problems over which they seemingly have little control. Curing rituals express people's desire to understand their fate, a truth succinctly expressed by a Navajo healer who was asked whether a patient cured of an illness by a Red Ant Chantway actually had had ants in his body. The healer replied: "No, not ants, but *ants*. We have to have a way of thinking strongly about disease." ▲

An Iroquois mask, worn during the Midwinter ceremony. Some recent Native American religious movements, including the Iroquois Handsome Lake religion, have inspired a resurgence in traditional religious practices.

REVELATIONS

Since the arrival of Europeans in North America, Native Americans have faced numerous hardships and suffered through countless individual and collective traumas. They have seen their lands taken from them, their communities destroyed by warfare and disease, and their lives controlled by foreign governments. In response to these disastrous changes in their circumstances, many Native Americans sought the help of the supernatural powers that they had traditionally relied on when in physical, social, or psychic crisis. In some instances, this developed into new religious movements that gained wide acceptance among the various tribes. Three such movements are especially notable for their large followings and their importance in the history and current lives of Native Americans. These include the Handsome Lake religion of the Iroquois, the Ghost Dance religion of the Plains Indians, and the Peyote religion of much of western North America.

The Handsome Lake religion was started by a Seneca man born in 1735 named Ganio-dai-io (Handsome Lake, in English) who lived in northwestern New York State. For the first 60 years of his life, Handsome Lake was a dissolute man who drank heavily and eventually suffered from severe alcoholism. In 1795, he was afflicted with a serious disease and was bedridden for four years, at which point he appeared to die. His family and friends gathered to attend his funeral, but Handsome Lake suddenly recovered, reporting that he had had a miraculous experience during his illness. He had been visited by four beings sent by the Creator, who had given him a message: The Creator was saddened by the bad actions of his people, but he was willing to give them another chance. The four beings gave Handsome Lake instructions from the Creator that when followed would make the people's lives prosperous and peaceful. The beings also told Handsome Lake, "The favor of the four beings is not alone for you and the Creator is willing to help all humankind," and they commanded him to transmit the Creator's message, called the Good Word, to the Senecas and to the five other tribes of the Iroquois Confederacy—the Mohawks, Oneidas, Onondagas, Cayugas, and Tuscaroras.

Until his death in 1815, Handsome Lake preached the Good Word among the various Iroquois settlements and received messages from the Creator. The Good Word, also called the Code of Handsome Lake, is now recited once a year at a thanksgiving ceremony conducted by people who have committed the text to memory. It begins with a narrative of events leading to Handsome Lake's visionary experience, including his illness and apparent death, and goes on to exhort the people to be kind to their elders, to treat children with patience and love, to avoid quarrels and malicious gossip, and to abstain from drinking alcohol. Spouses are urged to be faithful and to respect each other, and people are encouraged to cooperate and help others in times of need and to be generous, friendly, hospitable, and compassionate.

Aside from the recital of the Good Word, the Handsome Lake religion does not have special rituals. Instead, it encourages the practice of traditional Iroquois ceremonies, including the traditional thanksgiving and funeral rites and those conducted yearly at midwinter and at the planting and harvesting of crops. This affirmation of traditional Iroquois culture came at a crucial point in the confederacy's history. By the end of the 18th century, the Iroquois population had been halved by warfare and disease, and the confederacy had recently been the target of a devastating attack by American rebels during the revolutionary war. The Iroquois Confederacy had been weakened to the point of disintegration, but Handsome Lake's message of renewal and divine approval of traditional practices offered hope, encouragement, and unity to a demoralized population. In addition, Handsome Lake's espousal of temperance gained his movement the backing of local Christian groups and the written endorsement of President Thomas Jefferson (whom Handsome Lake visited in Washington, D.C., in 1802)—the first time a non-Christian Iroquois religious leader had been so encouraged. These honors were interpreted by many Iroquois to mean that they could exercise their traditional religious practices without the fear of reprisals from the United States, and the result was a resurgence of both interest and pride in Iroquois traditions.

After his death, Handsome Lake's disciples continued to carry the teachings of the new religion to all the Iroquois nations. By the early 20th century, adherents had established the Handsome Lake religion on every Iroquois reservation and reserve in both New York State and Canada. In some Iroquois

A young man recites the teachings and story of Handsome Lake in The Doctrine of Handsome Lake *by Seneca artist Ernest Smith.*

communities today, the majority of residents are members of the Handsome Lake religion, while in others, they comprise a small but influential minority. The influence of Handsome Lake's followers spreads beyond the religious community; they cultivate traditional Iroquois spiritual and social practices and play an active role in local and national Native American politics as ardent defenders of land and treaty rights.

Nearly a century after Handsome Lake received his revelation from the Creator, a Nevada Paiute man named Wovoka (1856–1932) had a similarly profound visionary experience. During a total eclipse of the sun on January 1, 1889, Wovoka (also known by his English name, Jack Wilson) was taken by spirits into heaven to meet with God. Wovoka later reported that

> When the sun died, I went up to heaven and saw God and all the people who had died a long time ago. God told me to come back and tell my people they must be good and love

Wovoka (left) was the Paiute prophet whose visions and teachings began the Ghost Dance religion.

> one another, and not fight, or steal, or lie. He gave me this dance to give to my people.

God told Wovoka that a new world was coming, where the living would be reunited with their deceased loved ones, where there would be no illness, and where there would be no old age. If people believed Wovoka's message and followed his teachings, they would be allowed to live in this new world, while the unbelievers would perish. Before sending Wovoka back to earth, God gave him powers to control the weather so that he could cause rain or drought at will. By using these extraordinary abilities, Wovoka showed people that his words were truly those of God.

Word of Wovoka spread among the Paiutes and other Nevada tribes, many of whom sent emissaries to him to determine if his teachings were proper and sacred. Many came away convinced, telling their tribespeople that Wovoka was the new Messiah or an incarnation of Jesus. Within a year, envoys were arriving from throughout the western United States and Canada and spreading the new religion with great enthusiasm when they returned home. A Cheyenne leader named Black Short Nose carried this message from Wovoka to his tribe:

> When you get home you have to make dance. You must dance four nights and one day time. Jack Wilson likes you all. His heart is full of gladness. I give you a good spirit. Be good always. It will give you satisfaction in your life. Every body will live again. There will be no sickness and all will return to young again.

In order to honor God and hasten the time of reunion with the dead, Wovoka instructed believers to perform special ceremonies, among them a type of dance called a round dance. Round dances are a traditional Native American ritual form in which men and women dance together in a circle while holding hands. Wovoka's dance, which became known as the Spirit Dance or the Ghost Dance, was conducted over a period of five nights and was sometimes the occasion for new visions of the spirit realm. Before the dance began, the ground was made sacred by sprinkling herbal powders on it. Participants adorned themselves with crow or eagle feathers and painted their faces with designs inspired by dreams and visions, often using red, yellow, green, and blue paint to make stylized images of suns, moons, stars, and birds.

A white American trader, J. F. Asay, described a Ghost Dance ritual that took place at the Teton Lakota community in Pine Ridge, South Dakota, in 1890:

> The dancers first stood in line facing the sun, while the leader, standing facing them, made a prayer and waved over their heads the "ghost stick," a staff about six feet long, trimmed with red cloth and feathers of the same color. After thus waving the stick over them, he faced the sun and made another prayer, after which

This 1891 hide, painted by Cheyenne artist Yellow Nose, shows Cheyennes and Arapahos performing the round dance that gave the Ghost Dance religion its name. The people lying down in the center of the circle have entered trances.

> the line closed up to form a circle around the tree [which had been placed in the dance ground] and the dance began. During the prayer a woman standing near the tree held out a pipe toward the sun, while another beside her held out four arrows from which the points had been removed.

As the religion spread to more tribes, new songs, prayers, and dances were added by local participants. These adaptations were often introduced following visions or dreams containing instructions from supernatural beings or were the result of local tribal customs being integrated into the basic Ghost Dance form.

Dances were accompanied by songs sung either by individuals or groups. These songs often dealt with the anticipated reunion with the dead and the coming of the new world. An Arapaho song states:

My children, my children
Look! the earth is about to move,
Look! the earth is about to move.
My father tells me so,
My father tells me so.

In one Lakota song, a mother sings of her expected reunion with her dead son:

I made moccasins for him,
I made moccasins for him,
For I love him,
For I love him.
To take to the orphan,
To take to the orphan.
Soon I shall see my child,
Soon I shall see my child,
Says your mother,
Says your mother.

The Ghost Dance religion emerged and spread at a time when traditional Native American practices were being suppressed by the U.S. government in an attempt to "Christianize" the Indians. Although the Ghost Dance religion contained certain Christian elements, it was decidedly non-Christian in its doctrine and observance, a fact that caused some consternation among white spectators. In addition, Wovoka prophesied the end of the world, at which time the earth would tremble mightily and the dead would be brought back to earth, led by a spirit figure in the shape of a misty cloud. While Wovoka informed believers that when "the earth shakes do not be afraid, it will not hurt you," the fate of nonbelievers and especially of whites in this prophecy was unclear—indeed, the prophecy appears to have come to different tribes in different forms. Some believed that after the cataclysm, all people would live in peace and friendship. Others believed that non-Indians would simply disappear from the continent, the buffalo and other game would return to roam the plains and prairies as they had before they were killed off by American soldiers and sportsmen, and Native Americans would resume their traditional lives. Still others believed that the cataclysm would kill off the whites in some horrible fashion—a belief that greatly concerned U.S. authorities, who feared that the Ghost Dance religion would inspire attacks on whites by Native Americans. This fear was decidedly irrational, since even in the most antiwhite version of the prophecy, the whites are killed by a divine cataclysm and not by vengeful Native Americans. Indeed, there is no evidence that Ghost Dance participants ever organized raids against whites, and Wovoka's doctrines were explicitly pacifist.

But the tension surrounding the Ghost Dance religion continued, reaching a deadly peak in 1890 on the Lakota reservations in North and South Dakota. The Lakotas, a powerful and populous tribe, had been removed to a fairly sizable reservation in 1868, but subsequent years had seen their territory broken up and drastically reduced as influential mining and railroad interests convinced the U.S. government to illegally hand over ownership of the Lakotas' land. To make matters worse, the buffalo population had been decimated by white hunters, U.S. authorities banned hunting on the reservations, and the harsh climate of the region stymied attempts to farm or ranch, making the Lakotas dependent upon U.S. government food rations to survive. These essential rations were drastically cut by authorities in the late 1880s, a period of especially severe weather that destroyed the crops. As a result, poverty, hunger, and disease were widespread, and death rates were correspondingly high. Not surprisingly, when Wovoka's message of a new world that contained plentiful game, had no whites, and reunited the living with their deceased loved ones reached the Lakotas in 1890, it was received enthusiastically throughout the reservation.

The U.S. authorities overseeing the reservation were considerably less enthusiastic. The Ghost Dance religion was not the Christianity preferred by U.S. officials, and to make things worse, the dance itself was often performed by large groups of people—one Lakota dance had over 2,000 participants—whom the authorities feared would use the opportunity to share grievances and plan uprisings. The U.S. government outlawed observance of the Ghost Dance religion on the Lakota reservations and threatened to imprison religious leaders and participants in Ghost Dance ceremonies, but in most areas the Ghost Dance continued unabated. Lakota leaders who were known to flout U.S. authority, especially the famous spiritual and military leader Sitting Bull, encouraged the performance of the dance in part to demonstrate their defiance of U.S. governance.

In November 1890, in response to repeated requests by Indian agent D. F. Royer (called Young-Man-Afraid-of-Lakotas by the tribe) and spurious rumors of a planned Lakota uprising, President Benjamin Harrison gave the secretary of war instructions to "suppress any threatened outbreak" of the Ghost Dance. Following these orders, more than 1,000 U.S. troops entered the Lakota reservations of Pine Ridge and Rosebud in South Dakota. Their presence drastically increased tensions on the reservations, causing thousands of Lakotas to flee their villages in anticipation of attack and resulting in a number of small clashes between soldiers and warriors. One such clash led to the tragic death of Sitting Bull, who was killed on December 15, during a shoot-out between his supporters and a police force sent to arrest him for his involvement in the Ghost Dance religion.

But the tragedy had just begun. The arrest of another Lakota leader, Big Foot, had also been ordered by General Nelson Miles, commander of the regional American army. At the time of the order, Big Foot was on his way to Pine Ridge to attend a meeting of Lakota leaders who hoped to negotiate a peaceful resolution of the crisis. Big Foot and his band of approximately 350 people (including slightly over 100 warriors) surrendered peacefully to a U.S. cavalry force of some 500 men on December 28, 1890, and set up camp at Wounded Knee Creek. Big Foot agreed that his band would surrender their weapons the next morning. By dawn, however, edgy U.S. forces had

A painting by an anonymous early 20th-century Lakota artist depicts the series of events that resulted in the death of Sitting Bull on December 15, 1890. The top right-hand corner shows Sitting Bull at a Ghost Dance pole praying, the center of the painting shows him being led out of his house by three policemen, and the lower left-hand corner shows the gunfight and resulting casualties.

set up four Hotchkiss guns—rapid-fire cannons that shoot explosive shells—to cover the encampment.

The surrender of weapons did not go smoothly, to say the least. Various warriors refused to give up their arms, and U.S. cavalry troops began a search of the tipis in the encampment, rifling through personal possessions and upsetting many families. A scuffle broke out between the warriors and the soldiers, and somewhere a shot rang out. The U.S. response was instantaneous and brutal. The Hotchkiss guns opened fire, killing over 200 people (including many of the hapless soldiers who had been searching the tipis) in a matter of minutes. Those Lakotas who attempted to flee the encampment were ruthlessly pursued and butchered by frenzied U.S. troops. (Lakota bodies were found as far as two miles from the encampment.) In addition, the Hotchkiss guns were reaimed and fired at the fleeing Lakotas. One eyewitness to the tragedy, a Lakota man named American Horse, described the scene:

> The women as they were fleeing with their babies were killed together, shot right through, and the women who were very heavy with child were also killed. All the Indians fled, and after most all of them had been killed a cry was made that those who were not killed or wounded should come forth and they would be safe. Little boys who were not wounded came out of their places of refuge, and as soon as they came in sight a number of soldiers surrounded them and butchered them there.

Over 300 people were killed at the massacre of Wounded Knee, approximately two-thirds of them women and children. The Lakota casualties (including Big Foot, who was killed in the initial burst of Hotchkiss fire) were buried in a mass grave by U.S. troops. Inquiries and public hearings were held investigating the massacre and detailing the deplorable living conditions of the Lakotas, but anti-Indian prejudice won the day—the commanding officer of the troops involved was exonerated and many of his soldiers were given medals for their so-called courage.

Another result of the massacre was the decline of the Ghost Dance religion among the Native Americans. Many advocates of the religion feared that if they performed the Ghost Dance, they too would be attacked by troops. This anxiety was so profound that when one ethnologist attempted to study the Ghost Dance religion among the Lakotas a year after the massacre, he was flatly told, "The dance was our religion, but the government sent soldiers to kill us on account of it. We will not talk any more about it." Small groups of followers from various tribes continued to perform the songs and round dances associated with the religion, however, emphasizing the good tidings of peace and righteous action instead of the prophecy of the world's end. Ghost Dance rituals are still held today, but their occurrence is infrequent and participation is limited.

Another Native American religion that developed in the late 19th century and has caused its share of controversy is the Peyote religion. Peyote—a small spineless cactus that contains mescaline and causes visual and aural hallucinations when eaten—has been used by Native Americans in Texas and Mexico (the growing range of the plant) since pre-Columbian times. In the 1870s, the use of peyote began to spread further north to the tribes of the Great Plains and to those tribes that had been removed to reservations in present-day Oklahoma. Although these tribes had not previously used peyote, many of them had traditionally consumed other plants with hallucinogenic qualities for religious purposes. Such plants are believed to possess significant spiritual power, as evidenced by their sometimes dramatic effects on humans. As objects of great power, they are also believed to be sentient, capable of hearing and responding to prayers, and able to provide those who consume them with valuable visions, spiritual understanding, and prophecies. Peyote's spiritual power is

A lieutenant of the 9th cavalry surveys the field after the massacre at Wounded Knee. Although the slaughter led to various governmental inquiries, the troops involved were never officially charged with any wrongdoing.

A Peyotist beats a ceremonial drum. During the 20th century, the Peyote religion spread widely among Native Americans.

such that, according to one Peyotist, "You can use Peyote all your life, but you'll never get to the end of what there is to be known from Peyote."

Although peyote is sometimes used illegally by non-Indians as a recreational drug, a Peyotist's purpose in consuming the plant is no more recreational than that of a Christian consuming communion wine. The effects of peyote are highly unpredictable and can be quite uncomfortable (strychninelike substances in the plant can cause painful muscle spasms and vomiting) or unpleasant (experiences of paranoia and depression are common). But no matter how disagreeable a peyote experience is, to a Peyotist it is always filled with religious meaning. Crashing Thunder, a Winnebago Peyotist, described an upsetting yet meaningful peyote experience in his autobiography:

> I tried to sleep. I suffered a great deal. I lay down in a very comfortable position. After a while a fear arose in me. I could not remain in that place, so I went out into the prairie, but here again I was seized with this fear. Finally I returned to a lodge near the one in which the peyote meeting was being held, and there I lay down alone. I feared that I might do something foolish to myself if I remained there alone, and I hoped that someone would come and talk to me. Then someone did come and talk to me, but I did not feel any better. . . . I went in [the peyote meeting lodge] and sat down. It was very hot and I felt as though I was going to die. I was very thirsty, but I feared to ask for water. I thought that I was surely going to die. I began to totter over. I died and my body was moved by another life. I began to move about and make signs. It was not myself doing it and I could not see it. At last it stood up. The eagle feathers and the gourds, these it said, were holy. . . . Not I, but my body standing there, had done the talking. After a while I returned to my normal condition. Some of the people present had been frightened thinking I had gone crazy. Others, on the other hand, liked it. It was discussed a great deal; they called it the "shaking state."

Peyote rituals, or meetings, follow a standard pattern, although certain elements may be adapted to suit the traditions of different groups or the individual visions of participants. Ceremonies take place in a tipi with a doorway facing east, the direction associated with the sacred power of the rising sun. Inside the tipi is an altar that holds traditional ritual paraphernalia such as eagle and crow feathers, gourd rattles, drums, bowls of water, and plates containing peyote buttons, as well as Christian religious paraphernalia such as crosses and Bibles. Meetings begin at sunset and end at sunrise the following morning. They are sponsored by a ritualist, called a road chief, who organizes the proceedings and supplies the peyote. During the meeting, members eat peyote buttons from a common plate and sing a peyote song, which may consist of standardized verses or of spontaneous lyrics revealed in visions. At dawn, a woman, usually the wife of the road chief, prepares a communal breakfast shared by all members.

The Peyote religion combines traditional Native American religious elements with those of Christianity. Not only is the ritual paraphernalia a mix of symbols from the two traditions, but peyote visions may be inspired by Jesus and angels as well as by traditional Native American spirits. Peyotists distinguish their practice from that of Christians, however, because they feel that they are able to obtain far more direct contact with the spirit world. In the words of the well-known turn-of-the-century Comanche chief and Peyotist Quanah Parker, "The white man

A delegation of Peyotists meet with a medical committee attempting to determine the legality of peyote in the state of Oklahoma in this 1907 photograph. Comanche chief Quanah Parker is seated in the front row, fourth from the right.

goes into his church and talks *about* Jesus, but the Indian goes into his tipi and talks *to* Jesus."

Almost as soon as the Peyote religion was introduced to the North American tribes, U.S. authorities attempted to stop the ritual use of the plant. In 1897, what was to be the first of many proposed federal laws that would outlaw the use of peyote in religious ceremonies came before Congress; it set the pattern for all such proposed federal laws when it failed to pass. In contrast, some state legislatures did pass laws banning all peyote use, and state and local authorities began arresting Peyotists, charging them with possession of illegal drugs. In response to mounting harassment, Peyotists legally established various tribal churches in the early 1900s, finally creating the intertribal Native American Church in 1918. By establishing a formal church, Peyotists hoped to obtain the legal protection to practice their religion as guaranteed by the freedom of religion clause of the First Amendment of the U.S. Constitution. But the controversy surrounding the use of peyote in religious ceremonies has continued throughout the 20th century.

Most recently, the U.S. Supreme Court issued a 1990 ruling, *Oregon Employment Division* v. *Smith,* concerning a state law in Oregon that declared peyote use and possession illegal without exempting religious uses. Two Native American Peyotists in Oregon had been fired from their jobs for using peyote in religious ceremonies and then were denied unemployment compensation by the state since they had been fired for participating in an illegal activity. Historically, the government has had to show that it had a "compelling state interest"—such as the preservation of life or property—before banning a particular religious practice, even if that practice is illegal in a secular context. In the 1990 ruling, however, the Supreme Court upheld the Oregon law, declaring that the government could restrict the practice of religion *without* demonstrating compelling interest if that practice violated federal or state laws (provided these laws were not specifically aimed at a particular religious practice). This broad ruling surprised even antipeyote groups (who had simply argued that the government did have a compelling interest in preventing all peyote use), because it essentially allowed for government interference in any and all religious practices. Indeed, in the majority opinion, Justice Antonin Scalia drew overt and favorable comparisons between the *Employment Division* case and the past legal prosecutions of Mormons for polygamy, and in a ruling immediately following the case, the Supreme Court recommended the overturning of a statute in another state that exempted the Amish (a religious group that believes modern technology is unholy) from current highway safety standards.

In response to these rulings, an unprecedented coalition of Native American, religious, and civil-liberties organizations covering the entire range of the political spectrum successfully

A group of Native American activists pose with President William Clinton (center) in the Oval Office on September 21, 1994, after the signing of the American Indian Religious Freedom Amendment.

lobbied Congress for the passage of the Religious Freedom Restoration Act, which was signed into law by President William Clinton on November 16, 1993. This law (which, as a federal statute concerning the Bill of Rights, applies on federal, state, and local levels) mandates not only that the government show a compelling interest whenever it restricts the exercise of religion but also that the government demonstrate that such constraints are the "least restrictive" means of fulfilling that interest. Less than a year later, President Clinton also signed into law the American Indian Religious Freedom Amendment, which explicitly guarantees the rights of Native Americans to practice their traditional religions, including the Peyote religion.

The teachings transmitted by adherents of the Handsome Lake religion, the Ghost Dance religion, and the Peyote religion are both novel and traditional. While new in a temporal sense, all these religious movements reinforced traditional beliefs and reflected traditional Native American philosophies and world views. Each religion developed and spread within a particular historical context, but each provided culturally familiar solace to people living in societies undergoing rapid, disastrous changes. Although these religions grew out of specific situations in Native American history, their appeal to the human desire to make sense of a world in turmoil, to make order out of chaos, is timeless and universal. Much like the older forms of Native American religions, the Handsome Lake, Ghost Dance, and Peyote religions instruct believers to look both inward and outward. By looking inward, people find the spiritual strength to cope with events in their lives, while by looking outward to others in their community, believers reinforce the collective bonds that have proven critical to the survival of Native American societies. Despite their obvious differences, all Native American religions carry a message of hope and renewal expressed in prayers and songs offered to the spirit realm—a similarity that prompted Lakota spiritual leader Lame Deer to declare, "I think when it comes right down to it, all the Indian religions are somehow part of the same belief, the same mystery." ▲

BIBLIOGRAPHY

Basso, Keith. *The Cibecue Apache.* New York: Holt, Rinehart & Winston, 1970.

Blackman, Margaret, ed. *During My Time: Florence Edenshaw Davidson, a Haida Woman.* Seattle: University of Washington Press, 1982.

Erdoes, Richard, and Alfonso Ortiz, eds. *American Indian Myths and Legends.* New York: Pantheon, 1984.

Fenton, William, ed. *Parker on the Iroquois. Book Two: The Code of Handsome Lake, the Seneca Prophet.* Syracuse, NY: Syracuse University Press, 1968.

Gill, Sam. *Native American Religions.* Belmont, CA: Wadsworth, 1982.

Hultkrantz, Ake. *Native Religions of North America.* New York: Harper & Row, 1987.

Jones, David, ed. *Sanapia: Comanche Medicine Woman.* New York: Holt, Rinehart & Winston, 1972.

Kehoe, Alice. *The Ghost Dance Religion.* New York: Holt, Rinehart & Winston, 1989.

La Barre, Weston. *The Peyote Cult.* 4th ed. Hamden, CT: Shoe String Press, 1976.

Neihardt, John, ed. *Black Elk Speaks.* Lincoln: University of Nebraska Press, 1961.

Ortiz, Alfonso. *The Tewa World: Space, Time, Being, and Becoming in a Pueblo Society.* Chicago: University of Chicago Press, 1969.

———, ed. *Southwest: Handbook of North American Indians.* Vol. 10. Washington, D.C.: Smithsonian Institute, 1983.

Spradley, James, ed. *Guests Never Leave Hungry: The Autobiography of James Sewid, a Kwakiutl Indian.* Montreal: McGill-Queen's University Press, 1972.

Sullivan, Lawrence, ed. *Native American Religions.* New York: Macmillan, 1987.

Tedlock, Dennis, and Barbara Tedlock, eds. *Teachings from the American Earth.* New York: Liveright, 1975.

Thompson, Stith, ed. *Tales of the North American Indians.* 1929. Reprint. Bloomington, IL: Indian University Press, 1966.

Tooker, Elisabeth. *The Iroquois Ceremonial of Midwinter.* Syracuse, NY: Syracuse University Press, 1970.

Underhill, Ruth. *Red Man's Religion.* Chicago: University of Chicago Press, 1965.

Walker, Deward, ed. *Witchcraft and Sorcery of the American Native Peoples.* Moscow: University of Idaho Press, 1989.

Wilson, Gilbert, ed. *Waheenee: An Indian Girl's Story as Told By Herself.* Norman: University of Oklahoma Press, 1981.

Witherspoon, Gary. *Navajo Kinship and Marriage.* Chicago: University of Chicago Press, 1975.

GLOSSARY

agent A person appointed by the Bureau of Indian Affairs to supervise U.S. government programs on a reservation and/or in a specific region.

American Indian Religious Freedom Amendment A 1994 federal law that explicitly guarantees the rights of Native Americans to practice their traditional religions, including the Peyote religion.

angakot A type of Inuit healer who helps retrieve people's souls when they have become separated from their bodies.

anthropologist A scientist who studies human beings and their culture.

culture The learned behavior of humans: nonbiological, socially taught activities; the way of life of a group of people.

dry paintings Images made with sand colored with different pigments used by the Navajos to help cure the sick.

Ghost Dance A ritual dance performed in conjunction with a messianic religious movement begun in the late 1880s by a Paiute man named Wovoka.

Hamatsa A secret society of the Kwakiutl tribe; also an annual renewal rite wherein a Hamatsa inductee is sent out to face a deity known as Cannibal Spirit.

Handsome Lake A Seneca prophet who in 1799 began a religious movement among the Iroquois Confederacy that resulted in a resurgence in traditional culture.

hozho A Navajo word meaning all that is good, favorable, desirable, beautiful, pleasant, peaceful, and harmonious.

itiwana The middle place of the world where the Zunis were told to settle after emerging from inside the earth, according to their creation legend.

kachinas Deities and souls of the dead who are impersonated in many southwestern tribes by people wearing special costumes and performing elaborate public dances.

kiva A special underground room where religious ceremonies are held among many southwestern tribes.

manitou A term for spirit power used by some northeastern tribes.

Midwinter A lengthy annual Iroquois renewal ceremony, which combines elements of thanksgiving, renewal, rejoicing, and preparation for the year ahead.

myth A story of an event in the prehistoric past. Myths often explain a practice, belief, or natural phenomenon.

nai'es The Western Apache puberty rite for girls.

Native American Church An intertribal Native American religious organization of Peyotists founded in 1919.

Oregon Employment Division* v. *Smith A 1990 U.S. Supreme Court decision that maintained that the government did not have to exempt religious observances when outlawing certain practices. The case, the result of a denial of unemployment benefits to two Native American Peyotists by the state of Oregon, was effectively overturned by Congress three years later with the passage of the Religious Freedom Restoration Act.

peyote A small spineless cactus that grows in northern Mexico and southern Texas and that causes hallucinations when ingested by humans. Peyote is considered a sacred plant by some Native Americans who consume it in special religious rituals.

Peyotist A person who believes that peyote has special spiritual powers and ingests it for religious purposes.

potlatch Ceremonial feasts held to commemorate special occasions among the costal tribes of the Northwest.

Religious Freedom Restoration Act The 1993 federal law that strictly curtailed the ability of government authorities to legally prosecute a person for conducting a religious practice that would be illegal in a secular context.

reservation A tract of land retained by Indians for their own occupation and use.

Sun Dance An annual renewal ceremony that is performed by many Great Plains tribes and is marked by dances and prayers.

sweat bath A ritual purification in a heated lodge filled with steam, often undertaken as preparation for contact with supernatural beings.

taboo A ritual restriction on a person's behavior

intended to protect from supernatural harm.

tribe A society consisting of several separate communities united by kinship, culture, language, and other social institutions, including clans, religious organizations, and warrior societies.

tricksters Characters in certain Native American legends who have special powers and who embody certain negative human personality traits.

vision quest A sacred ritual in which a person, often a teenage boy, is spiritually purified and goes off alone for a set period of fasting and praying in order to receive revelations from supernatural spirits, who may act as personal guardians.

wakan A term for spirit power generally used by the tribes of the Great Plains.

INDEX

PICTURE CREDITS

AP/Wide World Photos: pp. 35, 60; The Brooklyn Museum, accession number 03.325.3903, Museum Expedition 1903, Museum Collection Fund: p. 18; The Brooklyn Museum, accession number 05.588.7292, Museum Expedition 1905, Museum Collection Fund: p. 27; The Brooklyn Museum, accession number 11.694.9059, Museum Expedition 1911, Museum Collection Fund: frontispiece; California Historical Society, Title Insurance and Trust Photo Collection, Department of Special Collections, University of Southern California Library: p. 26; Canadian Museum of Civilizations: p. 66 (#91177); Copyright © Martha Cooper/Peter Arnold, Inc.: p. 52; Denver Art Museum: p. 54; Courtesy Department Library Services, American Museum of Natural History: pp. 15 (neg. no. 338014), 38 (neg. no. 35604), 47 (neg. no. 22866), 49 (neg. no. 326847), 78 (neg. no. 34048); The Eiteljorg Museum of American Indian and Western Art: p. 40; Field Museum of Natural History, Chicago: cover (neg. #A109069C); Fort Sill Museum, Fort Sill, OK: p. 92; Courtesy of the Iroquois Indian Museum, Howes Cave, NY: p. 24; Milwaukee Public Museum: pp. 37, 39, 41, 43, 44; Missouri Historical Society, St. Louis: p. 29; Nebraska State Historical Society: p. 89 (#W938:119-29); North Wind Picture Archives: p. 75; Photo by T. Harmon Parkhurst, Courtesy Museum of New Mexico: p. 30; Philadelphia Museum of Art: Purchased with funds from the American Museum of Photography: pp. 12, 32, 69, 90; Courtesy of the Royal British Columbia Museum, Victoria, British Columbia: p. 57 (#PN9689); Smithsonian Institution: pp. 58 (2372-A-4), 63 (3303-C), 84 (76-4941); Smithsonian Institution National Anthropological Archives, Bureau of American Ethnology Collection: p. 82 (1659-C); State Historical Society of North Dakota: p. 87; University of Pennsylvania Museum, Philadelphia: pp. 34 (neg # S4-141625), 42 (neg. # T4-516), 71 (neg. # S4-138293); UPI/Bettmann Newsphotos: p. 17; Photo courtesy of the U.S. Department of the Interior, Indian Arts and Crafts Board/The Heard Museum, Phoenix, Arizona: p. 81; The Wheelwright Museum of the American Indian: pp. 20 (P3A-#4A), 45 (P1A-#8), 73 (P20-#6); The White House: p. 94.

NANCY BONVILLAIN has a Ph.D. in anthropology from Columbia University. Dr. Bonvillain has written a grammar book and dictionary of the Mohawk language as well as *The Hopi* (1994), *Black Hawk* (1994), *The Inuit* (1995), and *The Zuni* (1995) for Chelsea House. She has recently finished work on *Women and Men: Cultural Constructs of Gender.*

FRANK W. PORTER III, general editor of INDIANS OF NORTH AMERICA, is director of the Chelsea House Foundation for American Indian Studies. He holds a B.A., M.A., and Ph.D. from the University of Maryland. He has done extensive research concerning the Indians of Maryland and Delaware and is the author of numerous articles on their history, archaeology, geography, and ethnography. He was formerly director of the Maryland Commission on Indian Affairs and American Indian Research and Resource Institute, Gettysburg, Pennsylvania, and he has received grants from the Delaware Humanities Forum, the Maryland Committee for the Humanities, the Ford Foundation, and the National Endowment for the Humanities, among others. Dr. Porter is the author of *The Bureau of Indian Affairs* in the Chelsea House KNOW YOUR GOVERNMENT series.